BUILDING A
CHAMBER MUSIC COLLECTION

A Descriptive Guide to Published Scores

by

Ella Marie Forsyth

The Scarecrow Press, Inc.
Metuchen, N.J., & London
1979

ML 128
.C4 F7

Library of Congress Cataloging in Publication Data

Forsyth, Ella Marie.
   Building a chamber music collection.

   Bibliography: p.
   Includes index.
   1. Chamber music--Bibliography. 2. Chamber music--
Analytical guides. I. Title.
ML128.C4F7   016.7857   79-4587
ISBN 0-8108-1215-0

PREFACE

The decision to create this selection aid was based on the writer's interest in chamber music, the assumption that there is an actual need for an evaluative selection tool for chamber music scores, and confidence that the writer could rely heavily on a specialized background as a professional clarinetist and teacher.

As a musician and teacher I was already familiar with much of the material represented in this guide, having either performed it or coached student performances. Although the bulk of the string quartet literature was familiar to me as a listener, I wanted to experience playing it, so I persuaded some string-playing compatriots to read through the basic literature with me while I transposed either the second violin part or the viola part on the clarinet. In this way I enabled myself to make better judgments. Although I have relied primarily on my own judgment for inclusion and placement of the works in the guide, I have consulted fellow musicians and standard reference sources at times on the appropriateness of those choices. With few exceptions, I have listened to each composition with score in hand. I felt this was necessary in order to develop a description, to determine how essential I thought each composition was, and then to place it in the priority arrangement. Needless to say, I expect disagreement with my choices but I would like to reiterate that it represents a personal selection.

The need for an evaluative tool was apparent in observing collections in which the standard repertoire was inadequately represented but in which there were many inferior or peripheral works. I started on this project assuming that most libraries could enhance their circulating music collections with chamber music in addition to solo literature. My assumption was strengthened when I read the following statement by two librarians who head fine arts and performing arts departments in public libraries.

"The library should probably continue to attempt
to serve the soloists and the small ensembles, the
advanced students and the accomplished laymen-
hobbyists with a rich variety of performance materials, chiefly because access to sources for either the purchase or borrowing of such materials is
often so very limited and difficult in many cities
of the United States and even more lacking in re-
tail music outlets than in bookstores. The purchase of music is at best a difficult matter. If
the library can provide it, it may well have a
real impact on local program activity, especially
if loan policies are liberal enough to allow ade-
quate time for study, rehearsal and performance"
(Hester Miller and Kurtz Myers, "Building a Non-
specialized Collection, " Library Trends, 23:3
[1975] 349-60).

TABLE OF CONTENTS

Table of Contents

INTRODUCTION

This guide describes over 300 published chamber-music compositions, divided into ten basic categories and subdivided, where necessary, by instrumentation. Divisions which are not subdivided are either too small or too diverse. Within each of the divisions or subdivisions the compositions are listed, not in the usual alphabetical/composer arrangement, but rather by priority of selection, beginning with the most essential to a basic collection and ending with the least essential.

The guide is primarily designed to assist in the selection and purchase of performing editions; however, it could serve also as a tool for the development of a basic chamber music collection of scores and/or recordings. The supplemental Annotated Bibliography could serve similarly in the development of a book collection of reference sources for chamber music.

In addition to providing a priority of purchase arrangement, the guide provides full title and publisher information, a description of each work based on characteristics such as style and structure, and a list of sources of musical analysis or commentary for each work. All of the sources listed can be found in the Annotated Bibliography.

In making a search for existing selection guides I found that many lists and catalogs of chamber music are available, but only a few are annotated and none could be considered a comprehensive or general selection aid.

The Music Library Association distributes Basic Music Collection lists for full scores, and reduction scores, or parts, for chamber music for strings, and chamber music for winds. These range from trios to octets. Basic information includes title, instrumentation, publisher, and price. The National Association of Schools of Music publishes A Basic Music Library which contains a section on study scores

for chamber music. Only composer and title are listed.
Other lists were found in Music in Public Libraries by Mc-
Colvin and Music Libraries by McColvin and Reeves. Anno-
tated lists found were in The Literature of the Woodwind
Quintet by Peters, A Handbook of Literature for the Flute
by Pellerite, Music Librarianship by Bryant and The Reed
Trio by Gillespie.   These titles are all in the Annotated
Bibliography.

　　The title by Bryant listed above offers a general but
small core collection with brief information on the composer
and/or the work, publisher, and price. Although limited in
scope, the title by Gillespie came closest to the type of
guide I wished to develop. I started with it as a model because of the detailed information on style and performance
considerations.

THE SCOPE OF THIS GUIDE

　　It was my desire to present as broad a scope as possible in regard to number and variety of instruments. Some
definitions of chamber music exclude the sonata literature
and also the literature for more than eight players; however,
I felt it would be helpful to encompass compositions for from
two to 13 players. Excluded were electronic music, aleatory
music, combinations for voices alone, solo music (as distinguished from sonatas) accompanied by keyboard (with a
few exceptions), ensembles for the same kinds of instruments
(with one exception), and ensembles requiring percussion instruments.   There are some excellent sources mentioned in
the Annotated Bibliography that could serve as purchasing
guides to some of these excluded ensembles, such as A
Teacher's Guide to the Literature of Brass Instruments by
Rasmussen, A Teacher's Guide to the Literature of Woodwind Instruments by Rasmussen, Ensemble Music for Wind
and Percussion Instruments by Heller, Blockflöten-Bibliographie by Alker, and Handbuch der Blockflöten-Literatur by
Winterfeld.   Two excellent sources for reviews of new music are the journals of the Music Library Association (Notes)
and the International Music Library Association (Fontes Artis
Musicae).   Numerous periodicals such as The Instrumental-
ist and Journal of the Harp Association contain reviews of
newly-published music. If one is not familiar with music
periodicals, the survey series of articles compiled and edited
for Notes by Charles E. Lindahl would be helpful. It is entitled "Music Periodicals" and includes both current and dis-

continued periodicals. The first article in the series, "Woodwind and Brass" appeared in the March 1976 issue, volume
32:3.

SELECTION CRITERIA

The basic criterion was musical worth--what was the
best available literature for a particular medium. Other
criteria were that the list should contain not only works of
the standard repertoire for which there will be an expected
demand, but also some meritorious works which have less
appeal; that there should be a balance in regard to instrumental combinations, levels of appeal, and technical requirements; and that the list should be well rounded in regard to
national schools and in regard to traditional and contemporary music.

Even though I had played much of the repertoire I was
considering and might have chosen works on a random basis,
I attempted a systematic procedure, studying lists of the output of individual composers, listening to the standard repertoire, and studying scores. The pattern of selection was arbitrary, based first on an approach by composer and then by
medium.

In attempting to include lesser-known composers, I
selected their works for more unusual instrumental combinations. In making choices from works of composers such as
Mozart or Beethoven, I selected those most appropriate to a
beginning collection, presuming that the library or individual
would move toward a goal of having the complete works. I
made representative choices for composers of large output
with an eye toward the purchase of the work in collections.

THE DESCRIPTIONS

The drawing up of guidelines for the descriptions, and
then writing them, proved to be the most challenging aspect
of this project. They needed to be brief, yet broad enough
to give a general idea of the work--but not so broad as to
become meaningless or trite. I wanted to achieve a balance
between details of form and a general summary of style,
avoiding details of analysis, especially in view of the references being supplied from the large amount of literature on
the more famous compositions. A list was made of charac-

teristics which could be drawn upon. These were: (1) tonal, harmonic, and rhythmic aspects, (2) structure, (3) style, (4) texture, (5) relation of instruments to one another in the general design, (6) performance problems, (7) alternate instrumentations, (8) general mood, (9) audience appeal, and (10) the general consensus on the work.

HOW TO USE THE GUIDE

The most important feature of the guide is its priority arrangement. Within each division or subdivision, the compositions are listed in the order in which they should be purchased. They may be found listed alphabetically by composer in the Composer Index. This arrangement seems to be more useful for collection building than one in which the compositions are listed by composer with only a priority index at the end.

The general arrangement of the main categories is a common one for chamber music--larger categories by number of instruments (with the exception of "Ensembles with voice") and subdivisions by instrumentation. The subdivisions used for trios, quartets, and quintets are listed below with their respective instrumentations (see Abbreviations, page xviii).

String trio (vln, vla, vc)
Piano trio (pf, vln, vc)
Wind trio (combination of either wood or brass winds)
Mixed trio (wind/string combination with or without pf)

String quartet (2 vlns, vla, vc)
Piano quartet (pf, vln, vla, vc)
Wind quartet see Wind trio
Mixed quartet see Mixed trio

String quintet (string combination, usually 2 vlns, 2 vlas, vc)
Piano quintet (pf, 2 vlns, vla, vc)
Wind quintet see Wind trio (usually fl, ob, cl, hn, bsn or 2 tpts, hn, 2 trbs)
Mixed quintet see Mixed trio

The third category, trio sonatas, represents chamber music prior to 1800. It is usually performed by four players, two on solo parts and two on the basso continuo part,

SAMPLE ENTRY

1 **2**   **3** **4** **5**
*MOZART   Quartet, [string, [K. 458, B flat major, **6**
               "Hunt." ⌐1784. ⌐Ded. Joseph Haydn. 27
               min. ⌐Adv. / ⌐Allegro vivace assai.
          7 ⌐(Menuetto) Moderato. ⌐Adagio. Allegro
               assai.   **8**

9 The opening bars of the quartet, in 6/8 meter, sound
like the call of the hunting horn. Its outer movements...
   10 Cobbett, vol. 2, 158 **11**
Parts: Breitkopf; Novello ⌐
Parts, collections: Bärenreiter; Kalmus; Peters 16 ⌐**12**
Score: Bärenreiter; Eulenberg ⌐ **13**

---

which is basically a bass line sketch for a harmonization.
It is usually played by a keyboard instrument with doubling
by a bass instrument such as violoncello; however, string
groups do play trio sonatas without the keyboard. The violoncello plays the bass line. It is appropriate here to call
attention to the wealth of available trio sonata literature.
It is a wonderful source of repertoire for intermediate level
chamber-music players. A comprehensive list of music in
publication may be found under the heading "Trio-Sonatas"
in String Music in Print by Margaret Farish, which is one
of the sources discussed in the Annotated Bibliography.

     Each entry in the main part of the guide (see Sample
Entry) consists of the following elements, numbered corres-
pondingly in the sample: (1) asterisk denoting core collection; (2) last name of composer; (3) title information, including instrumentation, opus or thematic catalog number, key,
and popular title; (4) year of composition or, with "Pub.,"
of publication; (5) person to whom dedicated; (6) approximate
duration; (7) level of difficulty; (8) movement names; (9) description which points out salient characteristics such as
mood, style, or performance considerations; (10) list of
sources named in the Annotated Bibliography with their page
numbers; (11) publishers (with editors in parentheses) and
edition numbers, if available; (12) publishers of parts in collections (with editors in parentheses); (13) publishers of
scores (with editors or other information in parentheses).

     Instrumentation follows the order on the score; how-
ever, if piano is included it is listed first unless the composition is for piano and one other instrument in which case
piano is listed last.

Dates given are dates found either on the scores, in thematic catalogs, or in sources such as Cobbett's Cyclopedia. If the date of composition is not available, the date of first publication is given. Dates are lacking for a few early works and for a few compositions where verification was not possible.

Timings were taken from the score whenever possible. Record labels, record jackets, thematic catalogs, and the BBC Chamber Music Catalog were used also. All timings are approximate since they depend upon tempi taken by the performers and the number of repeated passages observed or ignored.

The words chosen to indicate levels of difficulty have special meaning within the context of chamber music. "Easy" means that players who have developed to the point of being able to play in ensembles will find the music within their reach. "Intermediate" means that the material is in reach of string players learning to move into upper fingering positions and wind or piano players who have a good command of scales and fingering technic. The music may present problems to the individual but not to the ensemble. "Advanced" means that the average devotee, professional or amateur, is able to handle the material, the professional probably playing it well, the amateur getting through it satisfactorily. The plus sign after "Advanced" means that the work requires a high degree of skill and musicianship.

In the list of reference sources for each work, only the last names of the authors and page numbers are given. If an author is represented in the Annotated Bibliography by more than one title, an abbreviated title is given.

Publishing information supplied is taken largely from the indispensable String Music in Print by Farish and other repertoire lists of fairly recent date such as The Index of Clarinet Music by Wilkins, published in 1975. The term "parts" refers to the separate notation each player in an ensemble uses. "Parts, collections" refers to parts of several compositions by one or more composers bound together--e. g. , six quartets are published such that the first violin player's volume contains all six of the first violin parts, and likewise for the others. The term "score" here means the notation of all the parts of the ensemble arranged one underneath the other on different staves, enabling one to see all the parts at the same time.

If a score is not listed, it is either unavailable, as is the case with most duo-sonatas (where the piano part serves as a score, showing the second player's part above it), or information was unavailable.   As a rule, publishers of parts will be publishers of the scores as well.

The Annotated Bibliography is, in itself, a guide to literature on chamber music written, for the most part, in English or translated into English.   Many of the entries are directly related to the main part of the guide, being the critical essays or discussions listed as references in the descriptions.   Other sources listed are catalogs, bibliographies of particular repertoires, thematic catalogs, works on individual composers which contain discographies and/or bibliographies, and sources of publishing information.

The Directory of Publishers (which includes distributors as well) gives the most current address available at the time the guide was prepared.   In many cases there are cross references from publishers to distributors or from former publishers/distributors to current ones.

The Popular Title Index shows not only the popular names for musical works used in this guide but also other names by which the works may be known.

The Composer Index is an alphabetical arrangement by composer of all the works in the main part of the guide. Compositions by each composer are in alphabetical order, followed by their page numbers.   If several works by one composer have the same instrumentation and the same generic title, such as "sonata," they are arranged by opus or thematic catalog number.

The user of the guide may find it helpful if, out of the three hundred listed works, a nucleus or core collection were selected.   Each composition from this suggested core collection (outlined beginning on the next page) has an asterisk by the composer's name in the main listing.   String quartets appear first because they form the bulk of the repertoire and usually represent the highest artistic achievements of the composers.   Quintets and then trios follow because of the relative ease in either adding or taking away a player. The order is an arbitrary one, based primarily on perceived user demand for the standard repertoire.

CORE COLLECTION

ABBREVIATIONS

Instruments

bar	baritone
bsn	bassoon
cl	clarinet
dbl bass	double bass
fl	flute
hn	horn
ob	oboe
pf	pianoforte
picc	piccolo
tpt	trumpet
trb	trombone
vc	violoncello
vla	viola
vln	violin

Thematic catalogs

B.	Burghauser (Dvořák)
BWV(Bach-Werke-Verzeichnis)	Schmieder (Bach, J. S.)
D.	Deutsch (Schubert)
G.	Gérard (Boccherini)
Hob.	Hoboken (Haydn, J.)
K.	Köchel (Mozart, J. C. W. A.)
WoO(Werke ohne Opuszahl)	Kinsky (Beethoven)
Wq.	Wotquenne (Bach, C. P. E.)

Levels of difficulty

Adv.	Advanced
Adv. +	Advanced, virtuoso
Int.	Intermediate

Other

ad lib	ad libitum
Comm.	commissioned by
Ded.	dedication
min.	minutes
no.	number
op.	opus
posth.	posthumous
Pub.	published, publisher
rev.	revised, revision
vol.	volume

1 DUOS

WITH PIANO

STRING DUOS

*BEETHOVEN   Sonata, vln, pf, no. 9, op. 47, A major,
              "Kreutzer. " Pub. 1805. Ded. R. Kreutzer.
              35 min. Adv. + / Adagio sostenuto-Pres-
              to. Andante con variazioni. (Finale) Pres-
              to.

    A brilliant sonata requiring great virtuosity, it has been described in terms of a concerto. The slow introduction of the first movement hints at the theme whose development is coming. When the theme does appear it is in the minor mode instead of the expected major and in a Presto tempo. The whole movement has an improvisatory quality because the Presto is interrupted several times with Adagio interludes. The second movement variations are based on a theme that is one of the most poignant and intimate Beethoven wrote.

    Cobbett, vol. 1, 90-91   Scherman, 188
    Ferguson, 80-81   Tovey, Chamber Music,
    Robertson, 265-66   135-36
Parts: Augener (Kreisler); Fischer (Auer) 03758; Schott
    (Kreisler) 02651/3
Parts, collections: Augener (Kreisler); Fischer (Auer) L789;
    International (Francescatti, Joachim or Oistrakh); Peters
    (Joachim) 3031; Peters (Oistrakh) 9172A/B

*BEETHOVEN   Sonata, vln, pf, no. 5, op. 24, F major,
              "Spring. " Pub. 1801. Ded. Count Moritz
              von Fries. 23 min. Adv. / Allegro.
              Adagio molto espressivo. (Scherzo) Allegro
              molto. (Rondo) Allegro ma non troppo.

    Opus 23 and opus 24 were written as a pair; however, opus 23 has been relegated to obscurity, which Joseph

Szigeti laments in his sensitive article on the subject of
"favorites" in Scherman and Biancolli's Beethoven Companion.
The sonata was labeled by a publisher, probably because of
its mood.   It is full of good humor and is the first violin
sonata in which the composer wrote a Scherzo.   It is recommended that the library purchase the complete set of ten
sonatas found in the collections listed below.
       Cobbett, vol. 1, 89-90   Robertson, 263-64
       Ferguson, 77-78   Scherman, 181
   Parts: Fischer (Auer) 03385; Peters 4066; Schirmer L468
   Parts, collections: Augener (Kreisler); Fischer (Auer) L789;
       International (Francescatti, Joachim, Kreisler, or Ois-
       trakh); Peters (Joachim) 3031; Peters (Oistrakh) 9172A/B

*BEETHOVEN   Sonata, vc, pf, no. 3, op. 69, A major.
                 1807-08.   Ded. Baron von Bleichenstein.
                 25 min.   Adv. / Allegro ma non tanto.
                 (Scherzo) Allegro molto.   Adagio cantabile-
                 Allegro vivace.

       Of Beethoven's five cello sonatas, opus 69 is particu-
larly well-known.   It is heroic in style and has a memorable
syncopated Scherzo.   Unlike the two earlier sonatas (1797)
of opus 5, it has three movements instead of two and the
Adagio is placed at the beginning of the final movement instead of the first.   The two later sonatas (1815) of opus 102
become more involved thematically and more reflective.
Purchase of the set is recommended.
       Cowling, 128-31   Scherman, 191-94; 692-94;
       Ferguson, 82-85   962-63
   Parts: Augener; International (Rose)
   Parts, collections: Henle (Linde/Navarra) 252; Peters 748;
       Schirmer (Schultz) L810

*BRAHMS   Sonata, vln, pf, no. 3, op. 108, D minor.
                 Pub. 1889.   Ded. Hans von Bülow.   23 min.
                 Adv. / Allegro.   Adagio.   Un poco presto
                 e con sentimento.   Presto agitato.

       The sonata in D minor is more symphonic, more dra-
matic, than either op. 78 in G minor or op. 100 in A major.
The intense opening movement displays Brahms' unique use
of pedal point and syncopation.   In the Adagio movement the
violin spins a heartfelt theme which grows more anguished
with the use of double stops; throughout, the piano plays a
supportive role.   The Scherzo is as delicate as the Presto
is vehement.   The intensity of the Presto seems to strain

the resources of the instruments. Opus 78, based on
Brahms' song Regenlied is quite lyrical; opus 100 is simply
structured and of a tranquil nature. The thematic material
in both of these other violin sonatas seems to evolve with
remarkable fluidity. Purchase of the three is recommended.

    Cobbett, vol. 1, 166-67;   Ferguson, 179-80
       179   Keys, 57-58
    Drinker, 122-26   Mason, Brahms, 189-201
    Evans, vol. 2, 230-42

Parts: Augener (Jacobsen); Breitkopf; Fischer (Auer);
    Schirmer (Kneisel)
Parts, collections: Henle (Hiekel/Theopold/Röhrig) 194; In-
    ternational

*BRAHMS   Sonata, vc, pf, no. 1, op. 38, E minor.
                  Pub. 1866. Ded. Joseph Gansbacher. 25
                  min. Adv. / Allegro non troppo. Alle-
                  gretto quasi menuetto. Allegro.

A very lyrical piece, but one in which Brahms does
utilize many contrapuntal devices--the last movement is a
brilliant fugue, there is canonic treatment in the Menuetto,
and there are many fugato passages in the first movement.
The piano and cello have an equal share in developing the
cantilena themes of the first movement. In place of a slow
movement Brahms puts a lilting minuet that has a beguiling
Trio, made more effective by the octave doubling of the
melodic line. Of the two cello sonatas, opus 38 has more
immediate appeal than opus 99.

    Cobbett, vol. 1, 171-72   Ferguson, 180-82
    Drinker, 81-83   Keys, 58-60
    Evans, vol. 1, 179-84

Parts: Augener (Schroeder) 5116; Breitkopf; International
    (Rose); Peters (Klengel) 3897A; Schirmer (VanVliet/
    Hughes) L1411

BRAHMS   Sonata, vc, pf, no. 2, op. 99, F major.
                  1886. 25 min. Adv. / Allegro vivace.
                  Adagio affettuoso. Allegro passionato. Al-
                  legro molto.

Every movement has tremendous vigor. It is not a
tuneful sonata--the cello has a rather fragmentary and angular part. Both instruments have long passages of tremolo in
the first movement; there are dramatic pizzicato effects in
the second and fourth. The cello part requires projection to
hold its own with the virtuoso piano part. There are notable

shifts of tonality--the first movement, which begins in F major, moves to F sharp minor for the development.   There is a similar shift downward or upward in each of the other movements.

Cobbett, vol. 1, 177-78   Ferguson, 182-83
Colles, 148-49   Keys, 60
Drinker, 98-99   Mason, Brahms, 160-68
Evans, vol. 2, 172-83
Parts: Breitkopf; International (Rose); Peters (Klengel) 3897B; Schirmer 1889

*FRANCK   Sonata, vln, pf, A major.   1886.   33 min. Adv. / Allegretto ben moderato.   Allegro. (Recitativo-Fantasia) Ben moderato.   Allegretto poco mosso.

The structure is cyclic, with successive themes reappearing throughout.   Franck chose a sonata-allegro form for the second movement rather than for the first.   The work is intense and dramatic, requiring not only physical but also emotional endurance.   The piano part is quite difficult.

Cobbett, vol. 1, 424-26   Robertson, 276-78
Ferguson, 243-45
Parts: Durand; Fischer L766; International (Francescatti); Peters 3742; Schirmer (Lichtenberg) L1235

*DEBUSSY   Sonata, vln, pf. 1917.   14 min.   Adv. / Allegro vivo.   (Intermède) Fantasque et léger.   (Final) Très animé.

This sonata was Debussy's last work and characterizes his lucid textures and full palette of tonal color; it calls for delicate effects, especially in the second movement where the violin and the piano have reiterated staccato sixteenth notes.   Tonality is G minor.

Robertson, 279-80
Parts: Durand

*SCHUBERT   Sonata, vln, pf, op. posth.   162 (D. 574), A major, "Duo." Pub. 1851.   23 min. Int.-Adv. / Allegro moderato.   (Scherzo) Presto.   Andantino.   Allegro vivace.

Although not difficult technically, this sonata offers enough musical complexity and drama to warrant frequent appearances on recital programs.   The piano part has a

nice balance between melody, arpeggios, and chords. The
collections listed below contain the sonatinas, op. 137.

Cobbett, vol. 2, 355   Ferguson, 136
Einstein, Schubert, 133-   Westrup, 53-55
34
Parts: International; Peters 156BB
Parts, collections: Bärenreiter (Wirth); Universal Edition
(Oistrakh) 13308

*SCHUBERT   Sonatinas, vln, pf, op. posth. 137, no. 1
(D. 384), D major; no. 2 (D. 385), A
minor; no. 3 (D. 408), G minor. Pub.
1836. 14 to 23 min. Int.

These lovely pieces present no difficulties for either
piano or violin; the violin part remains in first position most
of the time and the keys are easy. Simple as they are,
they are played by concert artists because of their beauty.

Cobbett, vol. 2, 355   Westrup, 53-54
Ferguson, 136
Parts: Breitkopf; Fischer L420; Peters 156A; Schirmer
(David) L921

*SCHUBERT   Sonata, vc, pf, D. 821, A minor, "Arpeg-
gione." 1824. 20 min. Adv. / Allegro
moderato. Adagio. Allegretto.

This was written for the arpeggione, a now obsolete
six-stringed instrument with a fretted keyboard. It has been
transcribed for a number of instruments, including the clarinet, but is considered as part of the cello repertoire. The
cello part is often scored an octave higher than it sounds,
but most modern editions show it in the proper octave. The
last movement is a good showcase for bowing virtuosity.

Cowling, 132-33   Robertson, 269
Einstein, Schubert, 245   Westrup, 56-57
Parts: Breitkopf (Mulder); Editions Max Eschig (Fournier);
International (Rose); Peters 4623

MOZART   Sonata, vln, pf, K. 454, B flat major.
1784. Ded. Regina Strinasacchi. 24 min.
Adv. / Largo-Allegro. Andante. Allegretto.

Mozart wrote over two dozen violin sonatas. The last
three, K. 454, K. 481 in E flat major, and K. 526 in A
major, are considered the finest. In Mozart's early sonatas

the violin played a subordinate role, but eventually a real dialogue developed, as exemplified in this sonata. The Andante gives the violin an opportunity to rhapsodize, yet it remains intimate rather than dramatic in feeling.

Cobbett, vol. 2, 176-77   King, 39-40
Einstein, Mozart, 252-
    60

Parts: Schott (Kehr)
Parts, collections: Henle (Schmid/Lampe/Röhrig) 78/79 (21 sonatas); International (Flesch/Schnabel) (19 sonatas); Peters (Flesch/Schnabel) 3315; Ricordi ER59/60; Schirmer (Schradieck) L836 (18 sonatas)

J. S. BACH   Sonatas, vln, pf, BWV1014, B minor;
                    BWV1015, A major; BWV1016, E major;
                    BWV1017, C minor; BWV1018, F minor;
                    BWV1019, G major. 1717-23. 13 to 18
                    min. each. Adv.

These sonatas were not actually published until around 1800. They are structured in the sonata chiesa form (slow-fast-slow-fast), although the sonata in G major, an exceptionally beautiful one, does have five movements. The keyboard parts often consist of two independent voices weaving a contrapuntal texture with the violin. A string instrument may double the bass line.

Cobbett, vol. 1, 51-53   Robertson, 255-57
Ferguson, 25-27
Parts: Schirmer
Parts, collections: Bärenreiter (Gerber) 51189; Breitkopf (Naumann); Henle (Eppstein) 223; International (David); Peters (David) 232/33; Peters (Jacobsen) 232C/33C

BOCCHERINI   Sonatas, vc, pf, G. 8, B flat major; G. 14,
                    E flat major; G. 2b, C minor; G. 15, G
                    major; G. 11, E flat major; G. 17, C
                    major. 8 to 9 min. each. Int.

It is believed that Boccherini intended the cello part to be accompanied by a violin or double bass instead of a keyboard; Gérard suggests in his catalog that the accompaniment be as simple as possible and recommends the Schirmer edition. Movements are contrasting with monothematic structures.

Cowling, 115-118
Parts, collections: Ricordi (Piatti/Crepax); Schirmer (Bacon) L1874

DEBUSSY   Sonata, vc, pf. 1915. 20 min. Adv. /
                 (Prologue) Lent-Sostenuto e molto risoluto.
                 (Sérénade) Modérément animé, fantasque et
                 léger. (Final) Animé, léger et nerveux.

    The sonata has an improvisatory feel, with its many
tempo changes. It calls for a variety of bowing techniques.
In the second movement the cello must alternate between arco
and pizzicato rather quickly; there are passages where the
cello is made to sound like a guitar, and other passages
where a special effect is created by playing over the fingerboard ("sur la touche"). The second movement segues into
the third, which is cast in the classical sonata-allegro form.
The work ends in the key of D minor, its opening key.
        Cowling, 161   Robertson, 380-82
    Parts: Durand

HANDEL   Sonatas, vln, pf, op. 1, no. 3, A major;
                 no. 10, G minor; no. 12, F major; no. 13,
                 D major; no. 14, A major; no. 15, E major.
                 1700? 12 min. each. Int.

    There are 15 sonatas in opus 1; in addition to these
six, there are three for flute, four for recorder, and two
for oboe. Baroque sonatas are a rich source of training
repertoire and receive much use at the intermediate level.
The Schott edition shows the original figured bass as well
as a supplied one. It also includes a part for the cello ad
libitum.
        Cobbett, vol. 1, 508   Robertson, 257-59
    Parts, collections: Augener; International (Francescatti);
        Peters (Davisson) 4157A/B; Schott (Dofflein) 4326/27

RAVEL   Sonata, vln, pf. 1923-27. Ded. Hélène
                 Jourdan-Morhange. 20 min. Adv. / Alle-
                 gretto. (Blues) Moderato. (Perpetuum
                 mobile) Allegro.

    The texture is thin and the effect one of lightness;
the several themes of the first movement move freely between the piano and violin parts. The violin begins the Blues
movement alone with pizzicato chords which the piano assumes
later when the violin takes the tune. The last movement is
a continual series of sixteenth-note groups for the violin,
sometimes scale-wise, sometimes in arpeggios which shift
through many key regions; the work ends in a brilliant series
of double-stopped chords.

        Cobbett, vol. 2, 272-74   Myers, 75-76; 187-89
Parts: Durand

KODÁLY   Sonata, vc, pf, op. 4.   1909-10.   18 min.
                   Adv. / Fantasia.   Allegro con spirito.

    A two-movement work characterized as "impression-
istic." The cello begins the Fantasia alone and on a somber
note. The piano enters in an improvisatory manner and
this improvisatory quality is maintained throughout the movement. Momentum builds with an impassioned, ornamented
folk-like melody. After an agitated climax the piano pro-
duces harp effects leading to a somber ending. The second
movement is a dance which ends abruptly with a reappearance
of the somber opening of the first movement.
        Cobbett, vol. 2, 56-57   Cohn, Europe, 169
Parts: Universal Edition 7130

VIVALDI   Sonatas, vc, pf, op. 17, B flat major, A
                   minor, B flat major, E minor, B flat major.
                   1700? 10 min. each. Int.

    The movement names are the same for each sonata--
Largo, Allegro, Largo, Allegro. The sonatas present a
wide variety of melodic and rhythmic figurations, making
them excellent material for the student. Cowling believes
that these sonatas represent the best of the Italian Baroque
cello sonatas. With the revival of interest in Vivaldi, more
and more editions are coming out.
        Cowling, 91-92; 77-96   Ulrich, Chapter 5
        Tovey, Chamber Music,
          2-10
Parts, collections: International (Rose); International (Dal-
    lapiccola); Peters 4938; Schirmer (Graudan); Schott 4927

PROKOFIEV   Sonata, vc, pf, op. 119.   1949.   22 min.
                   Adv. / Andante grave.   Moderato.   Al-
                   legro ma non troppo.

    There are no stark contrasts, the outer movements
containing cantabile themes and the middle movement reminiscent of the Romeo and Juliet ballet score. The second
movement employs effective broken chords and pizzicato
double stops for the cello. The last movement has dramatic
sweeping effects in both parts.
        Cobbett, vol. 3, 140
Parts: International (Rostropovich); MCA; Peters 4710

SHOSTAKOVICH   Sonata, vc, pf, op. 40, D minor. 1934.
27 min. Adv. / Moderato. Moderato con
moto. Largo. Allegretto.

Composed along classical sonata lines; the first and
third movements are somber and sustained; the second and
fourth, crisp and light. The second-movement passages of
arpeggios played on harmonics require great skill on the
part of the cellist.
Cobbett, vol. 3, 143   Martynov, 55-57
Parts: International (Rose); MCA (Piatigorsky); Peters 4748

BARBER   Sonata, vc, pf, op. 6. 1932. 18 min.
Adv. / Allegro ma non troppo. Adagio-
Presto-Adagio. Allegro appassionato.

A lyrical sonata written in a romantic vein, it has
achieved universal acceptance and a place in the standard
literature. Thematic material is shared by both instruments.
The key signature is three flats, sometimes in the major
mode, sometimes in the minor. The second movement is
unusually structured--a tripartite form beginning and ending
with an Adagio in 4/4 meter and containing an Allegro in
12/8 meter in the middle. The sonata makes no unusual
demands on the players.
Cohn, Western Hemis-   Cowling, 161
phere, 20-21
Parts: Schirmer

FAURÉ   Sonata, vc, pf, op. 109, D minor. 1917.
20 min. Adv. / Allegro. Andante.
(Final) Allegro commodo.

Fauré's two cello sonatas are exquisite and should be
part of the sonata collection. The second one, opus 117,
was written in 1922. Fauré's style is very different from
most of the post-romantics of his time, whose scores are
thick, overblown, and uninspired. Fauré's harmonies are
rich, but he writes in a restrained, sensitive manner. The
parts are not awkward, the cello part mostly in a broad
style in the middle range of the instrument and the piano
part largely accompanimental, consisting of eighth- or sixteenth-note arpeggiations.
Cobbett, vol. 1, 390-91
Parts: Durand

PROKOFIEV   Sonata, vln, pf, op. 80, F minor. 1946.

29 min.   Adv.   /   Andante assai.   Allegro
brusco.   Andante.   Allegrissimo.

This is the composer's second violin sonata, the first
being a rearrangement of his flute sonata.   The first movement is rather somber; Prokofiev describes the second as
"impetuous and wild, yet with a broadly-flowing secondary
theme. "   Of the third movement, he states that it is "...
slow moving and mellow ... " while the fourth "... works
up to a frenzied impetus in a highly complicated metre.... "
    Cobbett, vol. 3, 139-40
Parts: International (Oistrakh); MCA (Szigeti); Peters (Ois-
    trakh) 4718.

HINDEMITH   Sonata, vla, pf. 1939. 22 min. Adv. /
              Breit, Mit Kraft. Sehr lebhaft. (Phantasie)
              Sehr langsam, frei. (Finale) Leicht bewegt.

Hindemith's two viola sonatas, this and an earlier one
from the 1920's (opus 11, no. 4, F major) are worthy contributions to the limited viola literature.   Both sonatas are
thick-textured and complex; however, the earlier has a more
flowing quality.   Its last two movements are highly chromatic
variations.
    Cobbett, vol. 1, 557-   Cobbett, vol. 3, 17-18
        58 (op. 11, no. 4)   (1939)
Parts: Schott 1976 (op. 11, no. 4); Schott 3640 (1939)

COWELL   Sonata, vln, pf, no. 1 (1945). Ded. Joseph
              Szigeti. 18 min. Adv. / Hymn. In
              Fuguing Style. Ballad. Jig. Finale.

There is a beautiful performance by Szigeti and Carlo
Bussotti on Columbia ML4841 Modern American Music series.
On the record jacket Cowell describes the sonata: "Both
the sonata and the short symphony begin with an introductory
hymn, then after the sonata-form fuguing movement they each
incorporate the Irish-American 'come-all-ye' ballad style for
their slow movements in song form and they have fiddle
tunes for their scherzos.   In the present work the piano and
violin contradict each other in canon at the start of the scherzos and play as if they hadn't properly started together at
several points.   The last movement focuses the forces ini-
tiated in the other four into a short and energetic statement
that falls apart just before the end as if momentarily dis-
tracted; then the music gathers itself together and broadens
to a full close that recalls the initial Hymn. "

Cohn, Western Hemisphere,
79-80
Parts: Associated Music Publishers

FINNEY   Sonata, vla, pf, no. 2.   c1971.   18 min.
                Adv. / Andante teneramente. Permuta-
                tions. Largo, teneramente. Allegro con
                moto.

An appealing contribution to the viola repertoire which
capitalizes on the tonal resources of the instrument; of moderate difficulty and with an even distribution of thematic material; texture is transparent; Finney frequently juxtaposes
tonalities. The distinctive title of the second movement describes the overall motivic treatment. There is an earlier
viola sonata in A minor.
Parts: Peters 66253

IVES   Sonatas, vln, pf, no. 1; no. 2; no. 3; no. 4.
                1908-15. 12 to 36 min. each. Adv.

Charles Ives' humor, innovations, and idiosyncrasies
are evident in the violin sonatas. There are long piano
solos/cadenzas and passages imitating bad piano players,
unusually structured movements, juxtaposed rhythms/meters,
shifts of meter, programmatic titles, and incorporation of
tunes and hymns that Ives heard as a boy. Distinctly American and distinctly original. Ives writes of the first sonata,
"... in part a general impression, a kind of reflection and
remembrance of the people's outdoor gatherings...." Of
the third, the longest (36 min.) and most complex, he writes,
"The first movement is a kind of magnified hymn of four
different verses, all ending with the same refrain. The
second may represent a meeting where the feet and the body,
as well as the voice, add to the excitement. The last movement is an experiment: the free fantasia is first. The
working-out develops into the themes, rather than from them.
The coda consists of the themes for the first time in their
entirety and in conjunction. As the tonality throughout is
supposed to take care of itself, there are no key signatures
...." The fourth sonata "Children's Day at the Camp Meeting" is a remembrance of summer camp meetings held in
New England farm towns between 1870 and 1900.
        Bader, 292-95   Cohn, Western Hemi-
                               sphere, 139-41
Parts: Associated Music Publishers (no. 4); New Music Edi-
        tion (Babitz/Dahl) (no. 3); Peer (no. 4); Schirmer (no. 2)

HINDEMITH   Sonata, dbl bass, pf. 1949. 15 min. Adv.
/ Allegretto. (Scherzo) Allegro assai.
Molto Adagio--Recitative-Lied--Allegretto
grazioso.

The sonata is characterized by utilitarian themes, a
piano part in a rather high tessitura, and a somewhat lighter
than usual texture. The first movement consists of a working out of two themes with skillful integration of the parts.
The bass has passages of pizzicato and harmonics. The
Scherzo opens with the theme in the bass with piano providing
staccato punctuation. When the bass moves on to another
contrasting theme, the piano begins a filigree accompaniment.
The first theme returns in abbreviated form. The Adagio
movement becomes increasingly florid and chromatic until it
becomes a recitative for both instruments which in turn leads
into a thinner-textured Lied.
Parts: Schott 4043

WIND DUOS WITH PIANO

J. S. BACH   Sonatas, fl, pf, BWV1030, B minor; BWV-
1031, E flat major; BWV1032, A minor;
BWV1033, C major; BWV1034, E minor;
BWV1035, E major. 1717-23. 8 to 16
min. each. Adv.

Movements are brief and alternate between fast and
slow; some doubt exists about the authenticity of BWV1031
and BWV1033. The first three were written with full harpsichord accompaniment, the last three with just the figured
bass. BWV1032 lacks a first movement. Editions vary
greatly in the realizations of the figured bass; the Peters is
recommended for less advanced students, the Bärenreiter for
those who need minimal editing.
Cobbett, vol. 1, 53-54   Ferguson, 26
Parts, collections: Bärenreiter; Boosey; Breitkopf; International; Peters; Schirmer
Score: Lea 10

BRAHMS   Sonatas, cl, pf, op. 120, no. 1, F minor;
no. 2, E flat major. Pub. 1895. 22 min.
Adv.

The first sonata is less lyrical than the second, its

opening theme broader and more angular than the flowing
theme of the second; the second movement of the F minor is
a tender, harmonically rich set of variations, while that of
the E flat major is an impetuous waltz. Both sonatas end
with a flourish of sweeping arpeggios; however, the F minor
has a truly dynamic Finale right from the start. Violists
consider the sonatas a part of their standard literature, also.
Some feel that the original instrumentation sounds better,
but the string instrument does have the advantage of a larger
variety of nuances.

    Cobbett, vol. 1, 181-82   Ferguson, 183-84
    Colles, 62-63   Keys, 66-67
    Drinker, 91   Mason, Brahms, 248-56
    Evans, vol. 2, 304-36
Parts: Breitkopf; Fischer; International; Peters 3896C.
    Viola: Augener; Breitkopf; International; Peters

HANDEL   Sonatas, fl, pf, op. 1, no. 1, E minor;
                  no. 2, G minor; no. 4, A minor; no. 5,
                  G major; no. 7, C major; no. 9, B minor;
                  no. 11, F major. 1700? 12 min. each.
                  Int.

    Handel designated three of the above sonatas for flute
and four for recorder. The recorder sonatas are published
separately by Peters. Those are no. 2, no. 4, no. 7, and
no. 11. The G minor, A minor, and F major are the easiest to play. Some editions include three early sonatas in
A minor, E minor, and B minor called the "Hallenser."
Peters publishes these separately. Most of the sonatas fall
into the "sonata da chiesa" form; however, the G major and C
major have five movements and the B minor has seven,
making them like suites. Parts may be played on a flute
or violin.

    Cobbett, vol. 1, 508   Robertson, 257-59
Parts, collections: Bärenreiter; International (Rampal) (10
    Sonatas); Peters (Woehl) 4552 (4 recorder), 4553 (3
    flute), 4554 ("Hallenser"); Schirmer (Moyse) (7 sonatas)
Score: Lea 70 (19 sonatas)

HANDEL   Sonatas, ob, pf, op. 1, no. 6, C minor;
                  no. 8, G minor. Pub. 1724. 12 min. each.
                  Int. to Adv.

    There are 15 sonatas in opus 1, six designated for
violin, two for oboe and the others for flute or recorder.
The oboe sonatas may be played by flute or violin. Each

of the sonatas has a fugal movement, a transitional Adagio, and a final dance movement. The dance movement of the C minor, a Bourée, is exceptionally brief.
Cobbett, vol. 1, 508
Parts: Associated Music Publishers (Glazer/Bodky) (op. 1, no. 8)
Parts, collections: Breitkopf; Peters; Ricordi
Score: Lea 70 (19 sonatas)

PROKOFIEV   Sonata, fl, pf, op. 94. 1943. 26 min. Adv. / Moderato. (Scherzo) Allegretto scherzando. Andante. Allegro con brio.

The opening movement contains two engaging themes in the neo-classic style associated with the composer. The second movement, a whimsical Scherzo, utilizes staccato in both parts for dry effects. The piano part is heavily textured in places and can overshadow the flute; flute figurations appear at extremes of the register which may cause problems in projection or tonal quality. The composer arranged this for violin three years later--it seems more telling on the string instrument. The International edition shows both flute part and violin on one score. Musica Rara furnishes a flute and a violin part.
Cobbett, vol. 3, 140
Parts: International; Musica Rara; Peters 4781 (violin)

PISTON   Sonata, fl, pf. 1930. Ded. Georges Laurent. 18 min. Adv. / Allegro moderato e grazioso. Adagio. Allegro vivace.

Piston has been described as a modern classicist, and this work demonstrates that classic balance between feeling and design. The individual parts are very active in a linear sense, working independently. The flute part moves into the lower register many times, requiring control and ability to project on the part of the flutist.
Parts: Associated Music Publishers

BEETHOVEN   Sonata, hn, pf, op. 17, F major. 1800. Ded. Baronin Josefine von Braun. 16 min. Adv. / Allegro moderato. Poco Adagio, quasi Andante. (Rondo) Allegro moderato.

The sonata displays the expressive rather than the brilliant qualities of the horn. Its themes are idiomatic, of necessity, since it was written for the natural horn. The

piano part is not difficult.   In three movements; the middle
movement is quite brief (actually an introduction to the Rondo)
and contains a little piano cadenza.
　　Robertson, 302
Parts: Breitkopf; International; Peters

HINDEMITH   Sonata, cl, pf.   1939.   19 min.   Adv.   /
　　　　　　　　　　 Mässig bewegt.   Lebhaft.   Sehr langsam.
　　　　　　　　　　 Kleines Rondo, gemächlich.

　　　　　　Overall, a finely crafted work in classical sonata
form.   The straightforward themes usually appear in the
clarinet part first.   There are many canonic, imitative passages.   All the movements, even the last, which is a jaunty
march, end on a tranquil note.   Parts are nicely balanced;
no excessive demands are made; not a hint of passion or
melancholy throughout.
　　Cohn, Europe, 109-10
Parts: Schott 3641

HINDEMITH   Sonata, bsn, pf. 1938.   9 min. Adv.   /
　　　　　　　　　　 With gentle motion.   Slow.   March.   Con-
　　　　　　　　　　 clusion, pastoral quiet.

　　　　　　A welcome addition to the sparse repertoire of bassoon sonatas.   The composer carefully avoids pitting the
thin, fragile sound of the bassoon against the piano.   The
overall effect is a bucolic one; each movement after the
opening segues into the next.
　　Cobbett, vol. 3, 18   Cohn, Europe, 108-9
Parts: Schott

HINDEMITH   Sonata, hn, pf. 1939.   19 min. Adv.   /
　　　　　　　　　　 Moderately fast.   With quiet motion.   Allegro.

　　　　　　The composer wrote two sonatas for horn, one for F
horn and one for E flat alto horn.   This sonata is for F
horn, which is more common today.   The later sonata (1943)
is for E flat horn, or mellophone.   Hindemith suggests that
the 1943 sonata be played on E flat alto saxophone as well.
It could also be played on baritone or tuba if transposed.
　　Cobbett, vol. 3, 20-21
Parts: Schott

HINDEMITH   Sonata, tpt, pf. 1939.   14 min. Adv.   /
　　　　　　　　　　 Mit Kraft.   Mässig bewegt.   (Trauer-musik)
　　　　　　　　　　 Sehr langsam (Alle Menschen müssen ster-
　　　　　　　　　　 ben) Sehr ruhig.

Hindemith stipulates that this may be played on the oboe, violin, viola, or clarinet, as well as trumpet. The composer advocated "Gebrauchsmusik," music intended for popular, informal use, rather than for concert use. His sonatas exhibit the traits of "Gebrauchsmusik"--forms of moderate length, moderate difficulty and with moderation of expression. The last movement of this sonata has an unusual opening, that of a funeral march. A more flowing, lyrical section replaces the march for awhile; then the march returns. The coda is a chorale melody. Trumpet in B flat.

  Cobbett, vol. 3, 19-20 Cohn, Europe, 111
Parts: Schott 3643

HINDEMITH Sonata, trb, pf. 1941. 14 min. Adv. /
      Allegro moderato maestoso. Allegretto
      grazioso. (Swashbuckler's Song) Allegro
      pesante. Allegro moderato maestoso.

Idiomatic writing at its best; the trombone part is mostly declamatory, but there are contrasting sections where agility is required. The sonata effectively displays the trombone quality in all of its registers. Themes are heard in both parts, but the main function of the piano part seems to be punctuation of the trombone statements.

  Cobbett, vol. 3, 19 Cohn, Europe, 110
Parts: Schott

HINDEMITH Sonata, bass tuba, pf. 1943. 12 min. Adv.
      / Allegro pesante. Allegro assai. Vari-
      ationem.

An engaging, witty showcase for double B flat or C tuba in three short movements, the first improvisatory in nature and the second a Scherzo with a brilliant decorative piano part in the upper range of the instrument. In the last movement the tuba presents the theme which is then treated contrapuntally in three voices, each hand of the pianist assuming a single, independent line. The final contrapuntal display of the theme, which is preceded by a long recitative for tuba, includes another filigree passage for piano. The ending is quiet.

  Cobbett, vol. 3, 20
Parts: Schott

POULENC Sonata, ob, pf. 1962. Ded. Arthur Honeg-
      ger. 14 min. Adv. / Elegie. Scherzo.
      Déploration.

Poulenc's affinity for certain harmonic progressions
and melodic sequences makes it impossible to mistake his
sonatas for any other's. The sonata movements are tripartite and without development, generally. The oboe's singing
quality and characteristic timbre are well suited to the mournful outer movements. The middle movement is a joyful
Scherzo in 6/8 meter with a poignant contrasting mid-section
in 4/4 meter.
Parts: Chester

POULENC   Sonata, fl, pf. Pub. 1958. Ded. E. Sprague
                 Coolidge. 13 min. Adv. / Allegro malin-
                 conico. Cantilena. Presto giocoso.

The first movement opens and closes with a lyrical,
romantic salon theme. Its middle section is an eclectically
treated classical theme. The second movement is similarly
"Poulencized" with a classical character and texture heightened with romanticism. The third movement is sprightly
and bustling, except for the legato interlude, and is typical
of the composer's tripartite movements.
Parts: Chester

POULENC   Sonata, cl, pf. 1962. Ded. Sergei Prokofi-
                 ev. 15 min. Adv. / Allegro. Romanza.
                 Allegro con fuoco.

In a record jacket note Edward Tatnall Canby calls
this "a tour-de-force of serious parody." It is quite appealing with its melancholic salon themes contrasting with those
filled with gusto and "joie de vivre."
Parts: Chester

SCHUMANN   Phantasiestücke (Fantasy-Pieces), cl, pf,
                 op. 73. Pub. 1849. 12 min. Adv. /
                 Zart und mit Ausdruck. Lebhaft, leicht.
                 Rasch und mit Feuer.

Lightweight and piano-dominated pieces which are
favorite program openers for cellists as well as clarinetists.
They may be played by cello, violin, or clarinet. Not particularly idiomatic for clarinet, but also without problems.
The piano part (which consists usually of half note chords in
the left hand and triplet arpeggiations in the right) and the
rather undistinguished melodic lines both contribute to a
sameness of sound. Each piece is in ABA song form. Clarinet in A; however, clarinetists often transpose the pieces on
B flat clarinet.

Parts: Peters (B flat or A); Schirmer (A)

SHAPERO   Sonata, tpt, pf. 1940.   Ded. Aaron Copland.
                     12 min. Adv.

       In this two movement (untitled) work Shapero writes
economically from a motivic standpoint.   He exploits just a
few intervals, combining and recombining them melodically
and harmonically.   The bulk of the sonata lies in the lively
second movement; the first movement, which features muted
trumpet against piano chords, is really a slow introduction
to the second.   Parts remain melodically independent; trumpet
alternates open and muted sound; obvious Copland/Hindemith
influence.
       Cobbett, vol. 3, 172
Parts: Southern Music

GALLIARD   Sonatas, trb, pf, no. 1, A minor; no. 2,
                     G major; no. 3, F major; no. 4, E minor;
                     no. 5, D minor; no. 6, C major.   1710?
                     10 min. each. Adv.

       These six sonatas, written for "low voice" are avail-
able also in an edition for bassoon.   The A minor and the
F major have been transcribed for double bass and the D
minor has been transcribed for tuba.   They are usually in
the slow-fast-slow-fast pattern.   The lovely melodic lines
show an Italian influence; the contrasting movements offer
ample opportunity to the player to demonstrate legato as well
as rapid articulation.
Parts, collections: Hinrichsen; International (bassoon and
       trombone); McGinnis and Marx (bassoon and trombone);
       Schott

---

(1) DUOS WITHOUT PIANO

*MOZART   Duets, vln, vla, K. 423, G major; K. 424,
                     B flat major. 1783.   15 to 18 min. each.
                     Adv.

       Of great artistic merit and beloved by string players,
these three-movement duets are a must for the collection.
The parts are beautifully balanced, giving the viola an equal

voice with the violin; the writing makes the two strings sound
like three or four at times.   Particularly striking is the
theme and variations movement from K. 424.

Cobbett, vol. 2, 166-67   King, 23-24
Einstein, Mozart, 185-   Landon, 135
86
Parts: Breitkopf; International (Gingold/Katims); Peters
1414; Schirmer (Doktor) L1827
Score: Lea 171 (with K. 563)

RAVEL   Sonata, vln, vc. 1920-22.   19 min.   Adv. +
                 / Allegro.   Très Vif.   Lent.   Vif, avec
                 entrain.

An exciting tour-de-force which utilizes many resources of string technique and Ravel's frequent compositional
device of cyclic form.   It is based largely on alternating the
major mode with the minor, and on consecutive major-seventh
intervals.   Each instrument has a proportionate share of the
accompanimental role.   The third movement is a fugue which
builds tremendous tension.   The whole work has a great
sense of propulsion.   The cello part is high and is written
a good part of the time in treble clef.

Cobbett, vol. 2, 272   Myers, 185-87
Demuth, 151-55   Stuckenschmidt, 194-95
Parts: Durand

KODÁLY   Duo, vln, vc, op. 7.   1914.   23 min.
                 Adv. + / Allegro serioso non troppo.
                 Adagio.   Maestoso e largamente-Presto.

A masterful work of lush tone color that draws on
Hungarian modal scales for its folk flavor and exciting rhapsodic passages.   In the first movement each instrument alternates between a melismatic vocal style and an accompanimental role, with beautiful dialogue between the instruments.
The second movement creates a mood of desolation reinforced
with tremolos and cello harmonics.   The last movement opens
with an accompanied violin cadenza and moves on to a Presto
dance for the rest of the movement.

Cobbett, vol. 2, 57-58   Cohn, Europe, 168
Parts: Universal Edition 7089

BARTÓK   44 Duos, 2 vlns.   1931.   2 min. each.   Int.

The composer wrote the duos to provide works suitable
for performance by students.   Songs and dances from many

countries are represented--all but two are based on peasant
melody; brief; polyphonically constructed.
Cobbett, vol. 3, 68   Stevens, 211-12
Cohn, Europe, 26   Ujfalussy, 305-7; 420-21
Parts: Boosey; Universal Edition

BEETHOVEN   Duets, cl, bsn, C major, F major, B flat
               major. Pub. 1810-15. 11 min. each.
               Adv.

The first two duets are structured similarly, with a
first movement in classical sonata form followed by a brief
slow movement, leading directly to a Rondo. The third duet
has an extended theme and variations for its second movement, followed by a quick coda. These are delightful to
play and make suitable recital music; they can be played
also by two clarinets or by clarinet and cello; arrangements
are available also for two strings; they can be taxing to
wind players because of the very few resting places.
Scherman, 43
Parts, wind: Associated Music Publishers; Hofmeister;
International; Marks
Parts, string: International (vln/vc or vln/vla); Peters
2523 (vln/vc)

MARTINŮ   Three Madrigals, vln, vla. 1949. Ded.
               Lillian and Joseph Fuchs. 15 min. Adv.
               / Poco allegro. Poco andante. Allegro.
               Moderato.

Diatonic; sonorous; idiomatic; contain many three and
four part effects with double stops and rapid alternations.
Cohn, Europe, 192
Parts: Boosey

PISTON   Duo, vla, vc. Pub. 1953. Ded. Sven and
               Kurt Reher. 15 min. Adv. / Allegro
               risoluto. Andante sereno. Allegro bril-
               lante.

A three-movement idiomatic work which makes a
decent contribution to the sparse repertoire for this combination. Parts are active, full of accidentals, and frequently
concerted. On one score, the individual parts are difficult
to read because of the close print; publisher does supply two
scores.
Parts: Associated Music Publishers

HINDEMITH   Duet, vla, vc. 1934.   5 min.   Adv.   /
                   Schnelle Achtel.

Employs a contrapuntal style with a small range of
intervals; alternating duple and triple measures throughout.
    Cobbett, vol. 3, 16
Parts: Schott 4765

TOCH   Divertimento, vln, vc, op. 37, no. 1.
                   1925.   Ded. Vienna String Quartet.   8 min.
                   Adv.   /   Flott.   (Intermezzo) Fliessend.
                   Frisch.

Themes are idiomatic to instrumental technique,
rather than vocal; a linear, polyphonic style without emphasis
on tonal color; of moderate difficulty--parts are "busy" with
long passages of eighth and sixteenth notes; no key signatures; much dovetailing of parts.   The duet won a prize
awarded by the publisher B. Schott's Söhne.   Toch, already
published by Schott, submitted the work anonymously.   Two
copies of the performing score should be purchased.
Parts: Schott 1910

TOCH   Divertimento, vln, vla, op. 37, no. 2.
                   1925.   Ded. Vienna String Quartet.   8 min.
                   Adv.   /   Vivace molto.   Adagio.   Flott und
                   lustig.

This duet possesses the same characteristics of the
duet, op. 37, no. 1, described above.   The first movement
is percussive and rapid, dominated by triplet figures moving
chromatically within a small range.   The last movement is
a vigorous one, built on a few rhythmic motifs.   Two scores
needed.
Parts: Schott 1909

JACOB   Miniature Suite, cl, vla.   Ded. Georgina
                   Dobrée and Anatole Mines.   1968.   10 min.
                   Int. to Adv.   /   March.   Berceuse.   Menuet
                   and Trio.   Fugue.

A delightful work which can be prepared quickly for a
program.
Parts: Musica Rara 1138

2 TRIOS

STRING

*MOZART   Divertimento, string trio, K. 563, E flat
major. 1788. 40 min. Adv. / Allegro.
Adagio. (Menuetto) Allegretto. Andante.
(Menuetto) Allegretto. Allegro.

A treasure trove for Mozart lovers, exhibiting Mozart's clarity of design. There is an even distribution of
motivic elements. The Andante movement begins quite simply
and proceeds through one beautiful elaboration after another;
the Menuetto movements are mindful of Haydn; the final Allegro is quite exhilarating.

Einstein, Mozart, 187-88   Robertson, 67-68
Parts: Breitkopf; International; Kalmus; Peters 1419
Score: Eulenberg (Peters E70); International

*BEETHOVEN   Trio, string, op. 9, no. 1, G major. 1796-
98. Ded. Count von Browne. 30 min.
Adv. / Adagio. Adagio ma non tanto e
cantabile. (Scherzo) Allegro. Presto.

The trios of op. 9 are masterpieces of the composer's
early period, displaying consummate skill in handling three
voices so that the texture never thins. The resources of
each player are drawn upon more than in quartet playing;
the Presto movement is full of challenging staccato passages.
Purchase of the Peters volume, which contains all the string
trios plus the trio op. 25 for flute, violin, and viola, is
recommended.

Ferguson, 92   Scherman, 229-31
Lam, 6-8
Parts: Breitkopf; International
Parts, collections: Peters 194 (with op. 3, op. 8, op. 25)

*BEETHOVEN   Trio, string, op. 9, no. 2, D major. 1796-

98. Ded. Count von Browne. 25 min.
Adv. / Allegretto. Andante quasi allegretto. (Menuetto) Allegro. (Rondo) Allegro.

This trio reflects the style of Mozart and Haydn. The
first movement follows traditional sonata form with a contrapuntal development on a rhythmic motif. The cello is
active in the last movement, introducing the theme and re-
maining in the high register a good part of the time.

Ferguson, 93   Scherman, 231-32
Lam, 8-10
Parts: Breitkopf; International
Parts, collections: Peters 194 (with op. 3, op. 8, op. 25)
Score: Eulenberg; Lea 99 (with op. 3, op. 8)

*BEETHOVEN   Trio, string, op. 9, no. 3, C minor. 1796-
              98. Ded. Count von Browne. 25 min.
              Adv. / Allegro con spirito. Adagio con
              espressione. (Scherzo) Allegro molto e
              vivace. (Finale) Presto.

The high point of op. 9 is no exception to the composer's use of C minor for his loftiest musical ideas. The
string parts are challenging and taxing; however, the artistic
results are magnificent.

Ferguson, 93   Scherman, 231-32
Lam, 8-10
Parts: Breitkopf; International
Parts, collections: Peters 194 (with op. 3, op. 8, op. 25)
Score: Eulenberg; Lea 99 (with op. 3, op. 8)

DVOŘÁK   Terzetto, 2 vlns, vla, op. 74 (B. 148), C
              major. Pub. 1887. 22 min. Adv. /
              (Introduzione) Allegro ma non troppo. Lar-
              ghetto. (Scherzo) Vivace. (Tema con Var-
              iazioni) Poco adagio.

Dvořák weaves the voices so skillfully that one hardly
misses the cello part; a must for the quartet player's library
for the occasions when the cellist is late. The Scherzo contains double stops in abundance and it has a "folk" feeling.
During the theme and variations movement Dvořák allows the
first violin a recitative passage against tremolo in the other
strings, which sounds as though he were thinking of a Mozart
opera.

Cobbett, vol. 1, 359   Sourek, 138-40
Parts: Artia; International; Simrock
Score: Artia; International

FRANÇAIX   Trio, string, C major. 1933. Ded. Etienne,
                  Pierre, and Jean Pasquier. 12 min. Adv.
                  / Allegretto vivo. Scherzo. Andante.
                  (Rondo) Vivo.

     A brilliant, sonorous work of attractive textures and
with characteristic Gallic élan. The first movement is a
teasingly brief perpetual motion with muted strings; the cello
part is full of leaping eighth-notes. The second
movement is a whirling waltz dizzy with syncopations and
which calls for much spiccato bowing. The third, also
muted, is a tender modal theme with a rocking accompaniment suggestive of a lullaby. The Finale, unlike the others,
changes moods, opening with a playful, bustling one and then
moving into a langorous interlude. After the original bustle
returns, the movement ends with a rollicking march.
Parts: Schott 3168
Score: Schott 3163

SCHOENBERG   Trio, string, op. 45. 1946. Comm. De-
                  partment of Music, Harvard University.
                  19 min. Adv. + / Part 1. 1st Episode.
                  Part 2. 2nd Episode. Part 3.

     Although extremely difficult, this is included because
it is a masterpiece of the form. A very personal work,
composed when Schoenberg was 71, it speaks to the listener
on intimate terms. There is discontinuity and violence in
it along with passages of moving lyrical tenderness. In a
single movement form of three parts separated by sections
called episodes. Coloristic ensemble textures; highly complex tonally.
     Cobbett, vol. 3, 3-5   Hymanson, 184-94
     Hill, 127-29   Whittall, 59-62
Parts: Bomart
Score: Bomart

FINE   Fantasia, string trio. 1957. 14 min.
                  Adv. / Adagio ma non troppo. (Scherzo)
                  Allegro molto ritmico. Lento assai.

     A moving and intense work with greater appeal than
many dodecaphonic compositions because it retains a linear,
unfragmented melodic style. The first movement, in legato
style throughout, begins with solo viola which is joined first
by violin and later by cello and develops into a marvel of
contrapuntal weaving. The Scherzo provides an abrupt contrast with percussive, syncopated, and rapid staccato and

spiccato passages; there are frequent pizzicato double stops
in cello.   The Lento is a return to a sustained style with
an arresting section in which the violin plays an impassioned
solo against sustained dissonant chords.
     Cohn, Western Hemi-
          sphere, 94
Parts: Mills
Score: Mills

TOCH   Trio, string, op. 63. Pub. 1955? 25
                min. Adv. / Allegro. Adagio. Allegro.

     There is a nice tribute to Toch, whose work is not
as well known as it should be, by Cohn in which he mentions
how Toch's music is spontaneous and constantly evolving,
without being driven into formal enclosures.   This trio reflects that freedom of structure.   Not easy to prepare; there
are many thick passages involving quite a bit of playing;
odd divisions of the beat and frequent meter changes.
     Cohn, Europe, 289
Parts: Associated Music Publishers
Score: Associated Music Publishers

TANEYEV   Trio, string, op. 21, D major. Pub.
                1909. 22 min. Adv. / Allegro giocoso
                e semplice. (Minuet) Allegro ma non trop-
                po. Andante. Vivace.

     Although Taneyev studied with Tchaikovsky, he wrote
in Mozartean style.   He was a master of counterpoint and
published the treatise Manual of Counterpoint in 1896.   Among
his other chamber music works are six string quartets and
a piano quintet.   At present op. 21 seems to be out of print;
however, there is an op. 31 trio in E flat major which is
available through International.
Parts: International (op. 31)
Score: Music Corporation of America

MOZART   Three Easy Trios, 2 vlns, vc, C major;
                D major; F major. 8 min. each. Int.

     Excellent material for beginning players; the movements
follow the general pattern of Allegro, Adagio, Menuetto, and
Rondo; the material is borrowed freely from other Mozart
pieces.
Parts: International (May)

MOZART   Trio, 2 vlns, vc, K. 271f (266), B flat

major. 6 min. Easy. / Adagio. (Menuetto) Allegretto.

This two-movement trio is another good introduction
to Mozart for the neophyte player.
Parts: Breitkopf; International; Peters V45 (incl. score)

J. C. BACH   Six Easy Trios, 2 vlns, vc, op. 4, B flat
                  major; A major; E flat major; G major; D
                  major; C major. 18 min. each. Int.

The trios are all two-movement forms--a slow movement followed by a minuet; inexpensive, quality introductory
material.
Parts: Heinrichshofen's Verlag (Höckner)

GIBBONS   Four Fantasies, string trio. Printed 1610.
                  4 min. each. Easy.

Composed originally for viols, these are instrumental
counterparts to the madrigal, the most popular secular form
of the period in which Gibbons flourished. Excellent for use
with students, especially because of the use of modal, rather
than diatonic scales; each Fantasy is marked Moderato.
Parts: Presser

---

(2) PIANO TRIOS

*MENDELSSOHN   Trio, pf, no. 1, op. 49, D minor. Pub.
                  1840. 35 min. Int. / Molto allegro ed
                  agitato. Andante con moto tranquillo.
                  (Scherzo) Leggiero e vivace. (Finale)
                  Allegro assai appassionato.

The themes are broad and mindful of Schubert song;
thematic substance equally distributed among the parts. The
Scherzo is typical of Mendelssohn's light touch; the Finale,
a brilliant one. Although op. 49 is slightly easier and recorded more often, both the trios (op. 66 in C minor) make
good pieces for the neophyte ensemble--the string
parts are relatively easy and the piano parts are
mostly arpeggiations.
          Cobbett, vol. 2, 133-34   Horton, 53-54
          Ferguson, 157-58   Robertson, 180-82

Parts: Durand; Schirmer L1458, L1459 (op. 66)
Parts, collections: Henle (Grossman) 250 (with op. 66);
    Peters 1740 (with op. 66)
Score: Eulenberg (Peters E80, E81 (op. 66))

*SCHUBERT   Trio, pf, no. 1, op. 99 (D. 898), B flat
                   major. Pub. 1836. 30 min. Adv. /
                   Allegro moderato. Andante un poco mosso.
                   (Scherzo) Allegro. (Rondo) Allegro vivace.

    The innumerable expressive themes reflect Schubert's
genius for song, the melodies often appearing as countermelodies to one another. Transparent textures and subtle
harmonic nuances; a demanding cello part; the last movement
contains great rhythmic variety as well as special effects
created by long tremolo passages for piano as well as for
strings. Schubert's piano trios provide the link between
those of Beethoven and those of the late Romantic period.
    Cobbett, vol. 2, 362   Robertson, 163-65
    Einstein, Schubert, 277-   Westrup, 47-50
      79
    Ferguson, 137-39
Parts: Breitkopf (Adamowski); Schirmer L1471; Universal
    Edition 4851
Parts, collections: Peters 167 (with op. 100)
Score: Eulenberg (Peters E84); Lea 110 (with op. 100, op.
    148); Universal Edition Ph379

*BRAHMS   Trio, pf, op. 8, rev. , B major. Pub.
                   1891. 32 min. Adv. / Allegro con brio.
                   (Scherzo) Allegro molto. Adagio. Allegro.

    The first version of this trio is a product of Brahms'
early years, the revised version of his mature years. It
is an impassioned work, calling for much doubling of parts
at the octave or in unison, which creates intonation hazards
for the players and a temptation to force the tone. There
is little contrast in tonality, every movement set in either
B major or B minor. The first Allegro begins with an arresting theme begun by cello and piano which gathers intensity
as it goes along. The Scherzo is based on a staccato theme
whose repetitions achieve a perpetual-motion effect; even
though the trio section is a lilting legato, it still carries the
momentum forward. The Adagio is a somber chorale with
dialogue between strings and piano--in the middle there is an
arresting cello solo in the minor mode. The Finale is rest-
less, dominated by its dotted rhythm opening motif.

Cobbett, vol. 1, 159-63   Keys, 41-50
Drinker, 55-60   Mason, Brahms, 3-12
Evans, vol. 1, 13-37   Tovey, Essays, 226-30
Ferguson, 184-86
Parts: Breitkopf; International; Peters 3899A; Schirmer L1514
Parts, collections: Henle 245 (with op. 87, op. 101)
Score: Eulenberg (Peters 246); Peters (Chamber Music of
Brahms, vol. 2)

*DVOŘÁK   Trio, pf, op. 90 (B. 166), E minor,
                 "Dumky." 1891. 32 min. Adv. / Lento
                 maestoso-Allegro quasi doppio movimento-
                 Poco adagio-Vivace non troppo. Andante-
                 Vivace non troppo. Andante moderato,
                 quasi tempo di marcia-Allegretto scherzando-
                 Meno mosso, allegro. Lento maestoso-
                 Vivace.

     Dvořák's use of the form of the Slavic folk ballad,
called a dumka, is a departure from the usual sonata-allegro
form; the multisectioned movements alternate between elegaic
and gay; many tempo changes to deal with as well as Dvořák's
tonal ambiguities.
     Cobbett, vol. 1, 369-70   Sourek, 161-68
     Ferguson, 230-32
Parts: Artia; Breitkopf; International; Simrock
Score: Artia; Eulenberg (Peters E332)

*HAYDN   Trio, pf, Hob. XV:25, G major, "Gypsy."
                 1795. Ded. Mrs. Schroeter. 16 min. /
                 Andante. Poco Adagio, Cantabile. (Rondo
                 all'Ongarese) Presto.

     There are now 45 piano trios available separately from
Doblinger, edited by H. C. Robbins-Landon. The series is
based on British authentic editions; editorial remarks are
published separately (Doblinger 13600) in English and German.
Each separate publication lists the incipits of all the trios
and carries a concordance of Hoboken and Landon numbers.
The smaller library may prefer the Peters three-volume
edition of 31 trios or the International edition of the five
most famous. The "Gypsy" trio, which takes its name from
the last movement, is the most famous trio (Peters no. 1)
and typifies the Haydn trio--an enlarged piano sonata in three
movements with strings adding color rather than participating
in thematic development. Written in Haydn's later years,
the trios should be considered as miniatures rather than minor

works. Fourteen of them (including no. 25), written between 1793 and 1796, are called the "London" trios.

Hughes, 146-49   Robertson, 41-43
Parts: Doblinger (Landon 39)
Parts, collections: International (5 Celebrated); Peters 192A/ B/C
Score: Lea 121/22/23/24 (31 trios)

HAYDN   Trio, pf, Hob. XV:24, D major.   1795.
                 Ded. Mrs. Schroeter.   15 min.   Int.   /
                 Allegro.   Andante.   Allegro, ma dolce.

Haydn dedicated three of his "London" trios (Hob. XV:24, XV:25, XV:26) to his intimate friend, Mrs. Schroeter. The first movement of this trio is very dramatic; the second is rather melancholic, with short phrases in minor; during this movement there is a rare cello statement of the theme while the piano and violin share an impassioned accompaniment; the last Allegro is more subdued than usual.   Landon no. 38; Peters, no. 6.

Hughes, 146-49
Parts: Doblinger (Landon 38)
Parts, collections: Peters 192A (12 Celebrated) /B/C
Score: Lea 121/22/23/24 (31 trios)

HAYDN   Trio, pf, Hob. XV:20, B flat major.   1794.
                 14 min.   Int.   /   Allegro.   Andante can-
                 tabile.   (Finale) Allegro.

Piano dominates and always states the theme first; the second movement is a lovely set of variations in which the violin participates fully; also, in the last movement the violin is given an arresting solo during an interlude in B flat minor.   As in many of the movements of the trios in the "London" set, there are modulations into distant keys. Landon, no. 34; Peters, no. 9.

Hughes, 146-49
Parts: Doblinger (Landon 34)
Parts, collections: Peters 192A (12 Celebrated) /B/C
Score: Lea 121/22/23/24 (31 trios)

HAYDN   Trio, pf, Hob. XV:27, C major.   1796.
                 Ded. Therese Jansen Bartolozzi.   18 min.
                 Int.   /   Allegro.   Andante.   (Finale) Presto.

A particularly brilliant trio with a multithemed first movement in which a rich development section in A flat major

is found. The Finale is quite gay--its opening motif is
worked over thoroughly; one of three (Hob. XV:27, XV:28,
XV:29) dedicated to Therese Jansen, a brilliant London
pianist. Landon, no. 43; Peters, no. 3.
    Hughes, 146-49
Parts: Doblinger (Landon 43)
Parts, collections: Peters 192A (12 Celebrated) /B/C
Score: Lea 121/22/23/24 (31 trios)

HAYDN   Trio, pf, Hob. XV:28, E major. 1797.
                    Ded. Therese Jansen Bartolozzi. 15 min.
                    Int. / Allegro moderato. Allegretto.
                    (Finale) Allegro.

    The middle trio of the three dedicated to Mrs. Barto-
lozzi is one of Haydn's most distinctive. The first movement, in a spirited mood, opens with a guitar effect, the
strings doubling piano notes pizzicato. The second movement is a contrapuntal throwback to Baroque style with an
arrestingly active bass line ("walking bass") and an unyielding
pulsation. The last is a very tender movement. Landon,
no. 44; Peters, no. 4.
    Hughes, 146-49
Parts: Doblinger (Landon 44)
Parts, collections: International (5 Celebrated); Peters 192A
    (12 Celebrated) /B/C
Score: Lea 121/22/23/24 (31 trios)

BEETHOVEN   Trio, pf, op. 1, no. 1, E flat major. 1793-94.
                    Ded. Count Lichnowsky. 24 min. Int. /
                    Allegro. Adagio cantabile. (Scherzo) Al-
                    legro assai. (Finale) Presto.

    Although the last of the three trios in op. 1, the C
minor, is considered the most significant, this trio is delightful and is frequently performed. The piano dominates
the first movement while the strings gain greater import in
the second. The third is an example of the composer's use
of a Scherzo instead of a Minuet in this position, and this
one is an impish one, based on a snappy grace-note figure.
The Finale is in the same high-spirited mood--its two playful
themes, the first on a motif of a leaping upward tenth interval and the second on a descending chord motif, lend themselves to extensive development; there are many brilliant
passages; in volume 1 of both Henle and Peters.
    Ferguson, 85-86   Scherman, 158-61
Parts: Breitkopf; Schirmer L1421

Parts, collections: Henle 24; International (6 Celebrated);
    Peters 166
Score: Eulenberg (Peters); Lea 151

SCHUBERT   Trio, pf, no. 2, op. 100 (D.929), E flat
               major. 1827. 40 min. Adv. / Allegro.
               Andante con moto. (Scherzo) Allegro mod-
               erato. Allegro moderato.

     The intense second movement is the emotional high
point. It opens with a march rhythm in the minor mode
which the piano lays as a foundation to a singular theme in
the cello. A second less intense theme then appears in the
major and builds up to a tremendous climax of sound. The
minor theme reappears for an even larger climax. The
movement ends with the excitement gradually subsiding into
a Coda echoing the minor theme. Schubert brings back these
themes in the final movement as part of the extensive development of its main themes, which themselves are highly
contrasting subjects, one in a 6/8 meter, the other in Alla
Breve. This trio does not "play itself"--it requires a sensitive performance to draw out its full beauty and to keep
it from seeming too long. The trio is less songful and more
dramatic than one would expect.
     Cobbett, vol. 2, 362   Einstein, Schubert, 277-80
     Ferguson, 137-39   Westrup, 50-53
Parts: Breitkopf; Schirmer (Adamowski) L1472
Parts, collections: Peters 167 (with op. 99)
Score: Eulenberg (Peters E85); Lea 110 (with op. 99, op.
     148)

BRAHMS   Trio, pf, op. 87, C major. 1882. 28 min.
               Adv. / Allegro. Andante con moto.
               (Scherzo) Presto. (Finale) Allegro giocoso.

     An appealing and straightforward work which is less
demanding and less complex than either the B major or the
C minor. The strings play long, singing lines, often in
unison. The second movement is a set of rhapsodic variations on a mournful theme, reminiscent of Hungarian folk
song; there is great contrast within the Scherzo movement
between the scampering effect of the opening and the lyrical
nature of the middle.
     Drinker, 77-80   Keys, 50-52
     Evans, vol. 2, 85-103   Mason, Brahms, 140-48
     Ferguson, 188-90
Parts: Breitkopf; International; Peters 3899C

Parts, collections: Henle 245 (with op. 8, op. 101)
Score: Peters 247; Peters (Chamber Music of Brahms, vol. 2)

BRAHMS   Trio, pf, op. 101, C minor. 1886. 22
                  min. Adv. / Allegro energico. Presto
                  non assai. Andante grazioso. Allegro
                  molto.

     The op. 101 is an extraordinary work which is not
performed as often as the trios op. 8 and op. 87. There
are unusual rhythmic subtleties as in the last movement,
which shifts from 3/4-2/4 meter to 9/8-6/8. There is
great transparency of texture, especially in the delicate second movement. The strings frequently function as a unit,
playing in unison or in the same rhythm. In the third movement there is a beautiful cello and violin duet alternating
with piano. The tranquil mood of this movement is enhanced
by rippling chords in the piano. Outer movements are vigorous; violin part is in a low tessitura and cello in a high
one a good part of the time.
     Cobbett, vol. 1, 177,   Ferguson, 190-91
       179   Keys, 52-53
     Drinker, 120-21   Mason, Brahms, 177-86
     Evans, vol. 2, 193-211
Parts: Breitkopf; International; Peters 3899D
Parts, collections: Henle 245 (with op. 8, op. 87)
Score: Eulenberg (Peters 248); Peters (Chamber Music of
     Brahms, vol. 2)

*BEETHOVEN   Trio, pf, no. 7, op. 97, B flat major,
                  "Archduke." 1811. Ded. Prince Rudolph,
                  Archduke of Austria. 35 min. Adv. /
                  Allegro moderato. (Scherzo) Allegro. An-
                  dante cantabile, ma pero con moto. Allegro
                  moderato-Presto.

     This last trio of Beethoven's is his most celebrated,
and rightly so, for the imaginative and spiritual levels it
reaches. It is filled with harmonic surprises and various
sound textures. The piano part is more difficult than the
string parts; the violin part is written in a relatively low
range. Purchase of the complete piano trios is recommended;
op. 97 is in volume 2 of both the Henle and Peters editions.
     Cobbett, vol. 1, 92   Robertson, 103-6
     Ferguson, 89-91   Scherman, 686-90
Parts: Breitkopf; Schirmer (Adamowski) L1427

Parts, collections: Henle 24/26/200; International (5 trios);
   Peters 166 (13 trios)
Score: Eulenberg (Peters); Lea 152 (with op. 1)

BEETHOVEN   Trios, pf, op. 70, no. 1, D major, "Ghost";
               no. 2, E flat major. 1808. Ded. Countess
               Marie von Erdödy. 26 min. each. Adv.

   Op. 70, no. 1 receives its nickname because of the
rumbling or murmuring effect of the first movement, created
by long tremolo passages and sixty-fourth notes in the piano
part. This movement is unique in its almost simultaneous
presentation of two themes and their almost simultaneous
development. The op. 70, no. 2 has been described as
amiable. A contributing factor may be that the second movement is a gavotte and the third a minuet; even the first movement has a dance quality with its 6/8 meter. The Gavotte
is a set of variations on two themes, one in minor, one in
major. The minor theme is based on a syncopated rhythmic
motif which is quite arresting. The last movement seems
weightier than the others and contains challenging rapid passages for each instrument.
      Ferguson, 87-89   Scherman, 680-86
   Parts: Breitkopf; Schirmer (Adamowski) L1426 (op. 70,
      no. 2)
   Parts, collections: Henle 26; International (op. 70, no. 1
      only); Peters 166
   Score: Eulenberg (Peters); Lea 152 (with op. 97)

MOZART   Trio, pf, no. 2, K. 502, B flat major.
               1786. 24 min. Int. / Allegro. Larghet-
               to. Allegretto.

   The Mozart trios are gems for the pianist--they are
concerto-like, with the string parts assuming minor roles;
the cello parts are particularly unventuresome. Although
this trio and K. 452 following are available separately, purchase of the seven piano trios in one volume is recommended.
      Cobbett, vol. 2, 169-70   King, 36-37
      Einstein, Mozart, 261
   Parts: Augener 7268B; Breitkopf; Schirmer L1603
   Parts, collections: Bärenreiter (Plath/Rehm) (16 trios);
      Henle (Lorenz) 247; International (David); Peters 193
   Score: Lea 49/50 (8 trios)

MOZART   Trio, pf, no. 3, K. 542, E major. 1788.
               20 min. Int. / Allegro. Andante gra-
               zioso. (Finale) Allegro.

This trio and K. 502 are considered masterpieces; this one is particularly pleasing because of its beautiful modulations and transparent textures.

Cobbett, vol. 2, 169-70   King, 36-37
Einstein, Mozart, 261
Parts: Augener 7268C; Breitkopf; Schirmer L1604
Parts, collections: Bärenreiter (Plath/Rehm) (16 trios);
Henle (Lorenz) 247; International (David); Peters 193
Score: Lea 49/50 (8 trios)

RAVEL   Trio, pf, A minor. Pub. 1915. 30 min.
          Adv. / Modéré. (Pantoum) Assez vif.
          (Passacaille) Très large. (Final) Animé.

The trio has immense appeal with its lush textures and contrasts of color and rhythms. The shimmering tremolos and sweeping arpeggios are orchestra effects reminiscent of his La Valse. The Pantoum is unique in its title and structure. Named after a Malayan verse structure, its form is a group of quatrains and each stanza in its first and third lines repeats lines two and four of the preceding stanza. Ravel shapes his musical phrases accordingly. The opening rhythm, therefore, is set in an unusual accent grouping within an 8/8 meter. There are other unusual rhythmic aspects, such as combining 3/4 meter in the string parts with 4/2 meter in the piano. The Passacaille is extremely effective, each instrument contributing equally to the dialogue.

Cobbett, vol. 2, 271-72   Myers, 181-85
Demuth, 143-51   Stuckenschmidt, 149-53
Parts: Durand
Score: Durand

SHOSTAKOVICH   Trio, pf, op. 67, E minor. 1944. 26
          min. Adv. / Andante-Moderato. Al-
          legro non troppo. Largo. Allegretto.

The first movement opening is unusual, beginning with cello harmonics that sound like the violin; when the violin enters softly, in its low register, it sounds like the cello. The movement gradually becomes more energetic and percussive. The second movement is humorous and buoyant which contrasts greatly with the third, a mournful one. The Finale opens with a pizzicato violin tune suggestive of a macabre dance--the movement closes quietly with a return of the first movement theme. This should have appeal even for those who shy away from 20th-century music.

Cobbett, vol. 3, 145   Martynov, 141-43

Parts: International; Music Corporation of America; Peters
    4744
Score: Universal Edition Ph181

DVOŘÁK   Trio, pf, op. 65 (B. 130), F minor. 1883.
                     40 min. Adv. /   Allegro ma non troppo.
                     Allegretto grazioso. Poco adagio. (Finale)
                     Allegro con brio.

      The mood of op. 65, with its mournful themes, is
consistently gloomier and more defiant than the well-known
op. 90 "Dumky" trio. It is typical, however, in its pianistic
style, key signatures of four and five sharps or flats, and
its chromatic harmonies. In each of the last three movements Dvořák creates a contrast of key and tempo at the
midway point, e. g. , the Finale is a scherzo in four flats
with a tranquil mid-section in four sharps.
      Cobbett, vol. 1, 365-66   Sourek, 153-60
      Ferguson, 228-29
Parts: Artia; International; Simrock
Score: Eulenberg (Peters E331)

TCHAIKOVSKY   Trio, pf, op. 50, A minor. 1882. Ded.
                     Nicholas Rubenstein. 42 min. Adv. /
                     Pezzo elegiaco. A. Tempo con variazione-
                     B. Variazioni, finale and coda.

      A "dust gatherer" due to its long-windedness and
virtuoso piano part. In spite of pleasing aspects, tedium
sets in with endless repetitions of themes in various keys
without thematic development. The composer was inspired
to write the trio on the death of Rubenstein, the great pianist
who was his friend. In spite of its title, the first movement
turns out to be rather robust. The second, and final movement, is a set of variations, divided into two sections, the
latter being the final variation and coda. The variations run
the gamut from a Mazurka to a Lament, and include a Fugue
along with the inevitable Waltz.
      Cobbett, vol. 2, 497-99   Ferguson, 224-25
Parts: International; Peters 3777
Score: Eulenberg (Peters E251)

---

(2) WIND TRIOS

BEETHOVEN   Trio, 2 obs, English hn, op. 87, C major.

Pub. 1806. 28 min. Adv. / Allegro.
Adagio cantabile. (Menuetto) Allegro molto
scherzo. (Finale) Presto.

A work in the style of Mozart, skillfully constructed.
As rich and sonorous as the double-reed timbre is, the trio
is not as appealing to general audiences as a string trio.
There is a companion piece for the same combination, the
variations which Beethoven wrote on the Mozart aria "La
ci darem la mano."
    Ferguson, 132-33   Scherman, 235-36
    Robertson, 303-4
Parts: Associated Music Publishers; Boosey; Costallat

POULENC   Sonata, tpt, hn, trb. 1922. Ded. Made-
                moiselle Raymonde Linossier. 9 min. Adv.
                / Allegro moderato, Grazioso. (Andante)
                Très lent. (Rondeau) Animé.

A work of great influence in brass ensemble composition; clashing intervals, bizarre effects, odd accents, a hint
of popular song here and there and a few titillating dance
sections provide a "tongue-in-cheek" style which requires
expert performers to bring off.
    Cobbett, vol. 2, 237   Cohn, Europe, 238-39
Parts: Chester

IBERT   Cinq pièces en trio, ob, cl, bsn. 1935.
                Ded. Fernand Oubradous, Trio d'Anches de
                Paris. 7 min. Int. / Allegro vivo.
                Andantino. Allegro assai. Andante. Al-
                legro quasi marziale.

These are similar in style to Ibert's pieces for woodwind quintet, which are light and entertaining. The clarinet
assumes a major role. The second movement is a duet for
clarinet and oboe.
    Gillespie, 41-42
Parts: L'Oiseau

MILHAUD   Suite d'après Corrette, ob, cl, bsn. 1937.
                12 min. Int. / Entrèe et rondeau. Tam-
                bourin. Musette. Sérénade. Fanfare.
                Rondeau. Menuets 1, 2, 3. Le coucou.

Most of the literature for this combination is French
and from the early 20th century; Milhaud's contributions,

this piece and a Pastorale, are perfectly suited to the combination. The suite is based on themes by an 18th-century
composer, Michel Corrette; Milhaud attempts to write in
that style, adding his own nuances and dissonances for flavor.
The oboe seems to be in the forefront most of the time.
    Gillespie, 53
Parts: L'Oiseau

BOZZA   Suite brève en trio, ob, cl, bsn, op. 67.
                Pub. 1947. Ded. Tony Aubin. 28 min.
                Adv. / Allegro moderato. Allegro vivo.
                Adagio espressivo. (Final) Allegro vivo.

    This makes demands on the players, but the result
is typical French elegance and fleetness. The harmonies reflect early 20th-century interest in modal and whole tone
scales, which create some reading problems for players.
There are many passages displaying the composer's command
of counterpoint. The oboe predominates.
    Gillespie, 24
Parts: Leduc; Musica Rara
Score: Leduc

FRANÇAIX   Divertissement, ob, cl, bsn. Pub. 1954.
                Ded. Trio André Dupont. 10 min. Adv.
                / Prélude. Allegretto assai. Élégie.
                Scherzo.

    A brilliant, yet whimsical tour-de-force with effective
but difficult repetitive patterns for bassoon and clarinet; key
signatures are challenging--the first movement is in five
flats, the last in six sharps; cross rhythms and jazzy syncopations; awkward intervals in the bassoon part. Clarinet
in A.
    Gillespie, 35
Parts: Schott 4331
Score: Schott 4268

PISTON   Three Pieces, fl, cl, bsn. 1925. 14 min.
                Adv. / Allegro scherzando. Lento. Al-
                legro.

    An early work, this ingratiating trio reflects Piston's
craftsmanship and precision. The outer movements are
structured on the fast-slow-fast principle; the middle movement, a Lento, features bassoon. A mood piece; ends on a
playful note with a distinct "Americana" flavor.
    Cohn, Western Hemisphere, 169

Parts: Associated Music Publishers
Score: Associated Music Publishers

ARNOLD   Divertimento, fl, ob, cl.   Pub. 1952.   9
                    min.   Adv.   /   Allegro energico.   Languido.
                    Vivace.   Andantino.   Maestoso.   Piacevole.

    Six short movements light in character and of moder-
ate difficulty with an even distribution of thematic material.
Arnold has written a jaunty woodwind quintet in the same
light vein called Three Shanties.
Parts: Paterson's Publications
Score: Paterson's Publications

TOCH   Sonatinetta, fl, cl, bsn, op. 84.   1954?
                    12 min.   Adv.   /   Allegretto commodo.
                    Slow, with utmost tenderness.   Allegro.

    A work to enhance the repertoire by a genuinely crea-
tive composer who does not resort to clichés.   The three
movements are in the fast-slow-fast pattern, with the middle
one featuring the flute; Toch writes the phrases in an over-
lapping style, with one instrument finishing a phrase begun
by another or with one instrument starting a new phrase before another finishes.   The piece needs careful counting.
Toch's career in Austria was interrupted by World War II
and resumed in Los Angeles, with the subsequent loss of
prestige encountered by so many émigré composers.   At
present the trio seems to be out of print; one hopes it will
reappear soon.
Parts: Mills
Score: Mills

LEEUWEN.   Eighteen Trios from the Classic Masters
                    for Two Flutes and Clarinet or Flute, Oboe
                    and Clarinet.   Ded. Georges Barrere.   3
                    to 4 min. each.   Int.

    A useful collection for beginning ensemble training,
it has compositions by Bach, Haydn, LeClair, Mozart, and
others.   Published in score form; the small print makes it
imperative for each player to have a score.   Other interesting intermediate-level wind music is available through Andraud or Southern Music (Texas).
Parts: Southern Music (Texas)

VILLA-LOBOS   Trio, ob, cl, bsn.   1921.   22 min.   Adv. +
                    /   Animé.   Languissament.   Vivo.

An effective display of the composer's complex distillation of Brazilian folk tunes and rhythms; harmonies associated with Debussy and Ravel; many changes of meter and
tempo with some difficult scale passages and large-interval
slurs in all parts.

Cohn, Western Hemi-   Robertson, 315
   sphere, 243
Parts: Eschig; International; Musica Rara
Score: Eschig; International

SEREBRIER   Suite Canina, ob, cl, bsn. 1957.   11 min.
                Adv. / Elegy to My Dead Dog.   Dance
                of the Fleas.   Transformation and Toccata.

The Uruguayan composer's work is tinged with humor
and enjoyable to play even though parts are difficult in places,
with rapid tongued passages, awkward trills, and leaps.   It
is complex rhythmically and very syncopated; a mixture of
atonality and Latin-American influences.

   Gillespie, 65
Parts: Southern Music
Score: Southern Music

RIISAGER   Conversazione, ob, cl, bsn, op. 26a.   Pub.
                1932.   8 min.   Adv. / Allegretto leg-
                giero.   Andante moderato.   Moderato-Alle-
                gro scherzando.

Riisager's work, especially his ballet scores, are
well known in Denmark.   His study with Roussel shows up
in the Gallic flavor.   The style here is concise; the crisp
outer movements are built on short motifs and phrases treated
imitatively while the inner movement is legato with more
sinuous lines.   Register extremes avoided.   Clarinet in A.

   Gillespie, 59
Parts: Engstroem & Soedring
Score: Engstroem & Soedring

SHAPERO   Three Pieces for Three Pieces, fl, cl, bsn.
                1939.   12 min.   Adv. / Classical.   Or-
                iental.   Contrapuntal.

A quite decent contribution to the sparse repertoire
for this combination; straightforward rhythmically and of moderate difficulty; the distinctive movement titles indicate the
style of each and show the composer's skillful handling of
the material; middle movement contains long cadenzas for

clarinet and for clarinet and flute; the last movement is made
up of three distinct fugal sections.
Parts: Peer International
Score: Peer International

MAREK   Trio, tpt, hn, trb.   1955.   9 min.   Adv.

A review in Brass Quarterly (3:3 [spring 1960]) describes this trio as a "most welcome addition" to the repertoire and refers not only to Marek's gift for fluent melody
but also to his skillful use of counterpoint. For those with
access to copies of Brass World there is a description by
Cramer of the work (4:1 [winter 1968], 326-28). In three
movements.
Parts: Robert King

---

(2) MIXED TRIOS

*BEETHOVEN   Trio, pf, cl, vc, op. 11, B flat major.
                1798.   Ded. Countess von Thun.   20 min.
                Adv. / Allegro con brio.   Adagio.
                (Tema: Pria ch'io l'impegno) Allegretto.

The opening movement is heroic in style with a brilliant piano part containing rapid scale passages and much
doubling at the octave; the part demands great delicacy as
well as power.   The Adagio is a heartfelt one, with cello
and then clarinet presenting the long song.   The theme and
variations movement is based on an opera theme and runs
the gamut of moods.   Generally, the clarinet and cello act
as partners, either taking turns at the theme or providing
embellishments to the piano statements.   Versions for violin,
cello and piano appear in the Henle, International, and Peters
editions of the piano trios.
        Ferguson, 87   Scherman, 163-64
Parts: Breitkopf; International; Peters 7064; Schirmer L1424
Score: Eulenberg (Peters E223)

*MOZART   Trio, pf, cl, vla, K. 498, E flat major,
                "Kegelstatt." 1786.   20 min.   Int.-Adv.   /
                Andante.   Menuetto.   Allegretto.

Mozart indicated that one of the parts was interchange-
able for violin or clarinet; however, it is generally agreed

that it properly belongs to the clarinet--the range and figurations are perfectly suited to it; also, the wind timbre adds
a distinctive color.   The work as a whole could be described
as flowing, intimate, and graceful.   It is difficult sometimes
to settle on a good tempo for the first movement and to agree
on the performance of the ornamental turn which figures so
prominently throughout the movement.

    Cobbett, vol. 2, 170   Ferguson, 53
    Einstein, Mozart, 261-   King, 35-36
      62
Parts: Breitkopf; Cundy; International; Peters R40; Schirmer
Score: Eulenberg (Peters E376); Peters R100

*BRAHMS   Trio, pf, cl, vc, op. 114, A minor.   Pub.
                1892.   25 min.   Adv. / Allegro.   Adagio.
                Andantino grazioso.   Allegro.

    Some consider this minor Brahms, others, usually
those who have played it, disagree.   There is less lyric
beauty in it than in some of the other works; one might say
that rhythmic and structural aspects come to the fore.   The
first movement opens with a broad theme stated first by
cello and then by the clarinet; cello also introduces the second theme, which is quite poignant; the coda is extraordinary
--the clarinet and cello play ascending and descending scale
passages at whisper level, the sound dies away and sets up
a hushed expectancy for the Adagio to come.   The Adagio is
lengthy, thick-textured, and taxing to the players, but the
artistic result is worth the strain.   The many passages in
unison create intonation hazards and the players have to refrain from slowing the tempo.   The third movement is a
lush waltz and the fourth a vigorous, driving Finale.   The
clarinet may be replaced by violin or viola; these alternate
parts are usually supplied by the publisher.   Clarinet in A
required.

    Cobbett, vol. 1, 180   Ferguson, 192
    Drinker, 45-48   Keys, 61-62
    Evans, vol. 2, 263-81   Mason, Brahms, 219-30
Parts: Breitkopf; International; Kalmus; Peters 3899E
Score: Eulenberg (Peters E250); Peters (Chamber Music
    of Brahms, vol. 2)

*BRAHMS   Trio, pf, hn, vln, op. 40, E flat major.
                Pub. 1868.   29 min.   Adv. / Andante.
                (Scherzo) Allegro.   Adagio mesto.   (Finale)
                Allegro con brio.

    How well Brahms met the challenge of writing a

melodic line for horn that would be suitable to the violin and
piano as well! He wrote magnificent parts for the horn in
this setting that match those in the orchestral settings. From
the broad opening theme throughout, there are lovely melodies.
The Adagio is particularly haunting. The Finale reminds us
of the hunter's horn and echoes the vitality of the chase.
Brahms wrote this for the "natural" horn, a valveless instrument, and much more difficult to control than the valve
horn. Piano and violin parts may be less demanding technically, but require a high degree of artistry.

> Cobbett, vol. 1, 172-73   Keys, 53
> Drinker, 111-15   Mason, Brahms, 77-86
> Evans, vol. 1, 185-203

Parts: Breitkopf; International; Peters 3899
Score: Eulenberg (Peters E259); Peters (Chamber Music of
   Brahms, vol. 2)

BARTÓK   Contrasts, pf, cl, vln, 1942. Comm. Benny
                Goodman. 18 min. Adv. / (Recruiting
                Dance) Verbunkos. (Relaxation) Pihenö.
                (Fast Dance) Sebes.

   Bartók, Goodman, and Szigeti played the first performance of this work, conceived as a two-movement piece,
but Bartók added the middle movement and gave it its present
title. The middle movement is very soft, with one climax
of sound in the middle--it is meant to convey "night" and
uses the violin and clarinet for color only--there is little
movement. The outer movements are brilliant, the first
one containing a highly-charged cadenza for the clarinet and
the third a virtuoso cadenza for violin. The entire piece
reflects Bartók's study of peasant folk music. The Recruiting
Dance employs the exotic rhythms and scales of Eastern
European folk music. The composer is economical and resourceful, shown here by the way he manages to explore new
textural colors with a traditional combination of instruments.
Clarinet in A and B flat; the violin player must either bring
two instruments or retune the one at an appropriate time,
because the third movement begins with the violin's outer
strings tuned to G sharp and E flat. When it is time to return to the normal tuning, Bartók instructs the piano and
clarinet to vamp while the violinist is retuning or changing
violins.

> Cobbett, vol. 3, 69-70   Stevens, 218-22
> Cohn, Europe, 28   Ujfalussy, 343-45
> Króo, 197-200

Parts: Boosey
Score: Boosey 723

DEBUSSY   Sonata, fl, vla, harp. 1915. 20 min.
             Adv. / Pastorale. Interlude. (Finale)
             Allegro moderato ma risoluto.

A remarkably refined work which exploits to the full-
est the individual instrumental sonorities; shows resourceful
use of the harp for dynamic and technical nuances on a level
with those of the viola and flute. Unlike Ravel's Introduction and Allegro of 1906 which may have inspired it, the
sonata fuses rather than contrasts timbre and stresses tone
color over brilliance. The Pastorale shows an aesthetic
balance of solo, imitative, and unison passages. The last
two movements are an exotic-sounding song and an exotic
dance.
        Cobbett, vol. 1, 319
Parts: Durand
Score: Durand

HAYDN   Trio, pf, fl, vc, Hob. XV:15, G major.
             Pub. 1790. 20 min. Int.-Adv. / Allegro.
             Andante. (Finale) Allegro moderato.

In the Collected Edition this trio and the trio Hob.
XV:16 are shown to be for flute, cello, and piano and the
trio Hob. XV:17 for flute or violin, cello, and piano; however, all three are played by both flutists and violinists.
The opening Allegro is vigorous; in it, as well as in the
other movements, the cello plays a supporting role to the
piano. These flute trios are really elaborate piano sonatas,
with the flute repeating or elaborating on the themes heard
first in the piano part. In the middle movement, which is
in song form, the piano has many ornamental passages and
the flute and piano play many scale passages in thirds or
sixths. The Finale is a delightful Rondo.
Parts: Doblinger (Landon 29)
Parts, collections: International (Rampal) (with Hob. XV:16,
    XV:17)

POULENC   Trio, pf, ob, bsn. 1926. Ded. Manuel
             deFalla. 14 min. Adv. / Presto. An-
             dante. Rondo.

Typical Poulenc in the elegant simplicity and tinge of
melancholy. Each movement is set up differently--the first
is declamatory, with the piano, then bassoon, and then oboe
in the forefront; the second movement is sustained and poetic,
with the piano functioning chiefly as accompaniment to the
lyrical lines of the winds; the Rondo is dance music, with

much interplay between winds and piano; lively staccato punctuations.
     Cobbett, vol. 2, 236-37   Cohn, Europe, 239
Parts: Chester

MILHAUD   Suite, pf, cl, vln. 1936. 20 min. Int. - Adv. / Overture. Divertissement. Jeu. Introduction et final.

     The first movement is noisy and gay, the second a tender lullaby. The third is a "busy" duet for clarinet and violin alone; the last imitates jazz in many parts. Melodies are diatonic; however, Milhaud likes to combine different keys. The individual lines are less interesting in themselves than in the way they combine with each other. This is an easy piece to prepare for performance and it has great audience appeal.
     Cohn, Europe, 215-16
Parts: Editions Salabert

MARTINŮ   Trio, pf, fl, vc. 1944. 18 min. Adv. / Poco allegretto. Adagio. Andante-Allegretto scherzando.

     French music from a Czech composer--Martinů lived in France and studied with Roussel. The first movement is like a nursery rhyme, playful and transparent. The last has the same child-like style, opening and closing with a march mindful of parade music. The cello part may be played on viola; it is necessary to request the extra part from the publisher.
Parts: Associated Music Publishers

IVES   Largo, pf, cl, vln. 1901. 6 min. Adv.

     A serious piece, with no humorous interjections. The piano part is complex rhythmically. It opens with a violin presentation of the motif; the clarinet assumes more importance in the middle of the piece and the violin again comes to the forefront at the end.
Parts: Southern Music

STRAVINSKY   L'Histoire du Soldat (The Soldier's Tale), pf, cl, vln. 1918 (original). 1924 (rev. original). 15 min. Adv. / The Soldier's March. The Soldier's Tale. A Little Concert. Tango-Waltz-Ragtime. The Devil's Dance.

The composer arranged this from his original score of the piece for theater. It is narrative music--the movement titles convey the story somewhat. The violinist plays double stops frequently; the clarinet part is in the high register many times, but is not as difficult as it may look; the meter changes may be problematic; the piano part is not demanding. Clarinet in A required.
Parts: Chester; International

REGER   Serenade, fl, vln, vla, op. 141a, G major. 1915. 17 min. Adv. / Vivace. Larghetto. Presto.

A very appealing romantic work in an almost classical style. Each of the cheerful outer movements contrasts a perky theme with a slower tranquil one. The Larghetto is a skillful polyphonic weave of the sound fabric; however, the thematic material is somewhat undistinguished. In this trio, a violin may substitute for flute--the Peters edition provides an alternate part. There is a companion trio, op. 141b, for violin, viola, and cello.
Parts: Peters 3453A

BRUCH   Acht Stücke (Eight Pieces), pf, cl, vla, op. 83, no. 1, A minor; no. 2, B minor; no. 3, C sharp minor; no. 4, D minor; no. 5, F minor; no. 6, G minor; no. 7, B major; no. 8, E flat minor. 1910. 3 to 5 min. each. Adv.

These romantic pieces give the pianist a chance to display some virtuosity; they are somewhat saccharine and may create monotony if heard in entirety; however, a group of two or three can be very effective; e. g. , no. 4 and no. 5 combine well. Nos. 1, 3, 5, 6, 8 are slow; nos. 2, 4, 7 are lively. Parts are furnished for clarinet/violin and viola/cello, offering a variety of instrumentation.
Cobbett, vol. 1, 215
Parts: Associated Music Publishers; Simrock

SCHUMANN   Märchenerzählungen (Fairy Tales), pf, cl, vla, op. 132. 1853. 14 min. Adv. / Lebhaft, nicht zu schnell. Lebhaft und sehr markirt. Ruhiges Tempo, mit zartem Ausdruck. Lebhaft, sehr markirt.

Although this is part of the standard repertoire, there

is nothing distinguished about the work, with the exception of
the poignant, song-like third movement which rises to a
greater expressive level.   It is accompanied throughout by
a rocking sixteenth note figuration in the piano.   Sensitive
performers can make the work seem first-rate.   Violin may
substitute for clarinet--an alternate part is usually furnished
by the publisher.
        Cobbett, vol. 2, 386
        Parts: Breitkopf; Cundy; International
        Score: Eulenberg (Peters E228)

KHACHATURIAN   Trio, pf, cl, vln.   1932.   18 min.   Adv.
                / Andante con dolore, con molto espres-
                sione.   Allegro.   Moderato.

        An attractive but uneven work with a strong nationalis-
tic cast.   The folk element is evident in the exotic harmonic
coloring and highly ornamented melodies.
        Cobbett, vol. 3, 140-41
        Parts: Breitkopf; International; Music Corporation of Amer-
            ica; Peters 5725

DAHL   Concerto a tré, cl, vln, vc.   1947.   20
                min.   Adv. +

        This one movement piece is based on a thematic germ
of six notes which appears in many harmonic and melodic
guises; its character is concertante and playful, with each
part rhythmically independent.   It begins in E flat major,
in an Allegretto tempo which changes to a tranquil mood in
the middle section.   Here there are many special string effects, double stops, and harmonics.   The clarinet leads back
to the opening theme with a cadenza.   After some more development of the motif, the work ends with a breathtaking
Presto.   The challenge to the performers is in maintaining
rhythmic independence and being able to sustain concentration without the usual pauses between movements.
        Parts: Boonin; Southern Music (Texas)
        Score: Boonin; Southern Music (Texas)

KELTERBORN   Lyrische Kammermusik (Lyric Chamber
                Music), cl, vln, vla.   1960.   12 min.   Adv.
                / Elegie.   Serenata.   Notturno.   Intermez-
                zo.   Nachklang.

        Five brief movements in atonal style; the dynamic
level is generally very soft, but within that framework there

are varying levels of excitement. Pointillistic effects; many long notes, beginning at different times for each instrument and creating a "layering" effect of sound. An excellent piece to program where contrast of instrumentation or a nod in the direction of contemporary music is desirable.

Parts: Bärenreiter 3477
Score: Bärenreiter 47

3 TRIO SONATAS

J. S. BACH   Sonata, 2 vlns, continuo, BWV1037, C
                  major. 1717-23. 12 min. Int. / Adagio.
                  Alla breve. Largo. (Gigue) Presto.

Trio sonatas offer a vast literature for the player at
intermediate level. The selections in this guide are only
representatives of hundreds of similar compositions by dozens
of composers. One need only consult String Music in Print
by Farish to see the possibilities for purchase. Most of the
sonatas fall into the sonata da chiesa pattern of slow-fast-slow-
fast or are suites or divertimenti with movement names
such as Prelude, Allemande, Gigue, etc. The sonatas are
usually played by four players, two on solo parts, one on
the keyboard part and one doubling the bass line of the keyboard on cello or another string. Many times the upper
parts may be played by flute, oboe, or violin. This trio
sonata in C major is fairly well known--its Gigue is a delightful canon.
      Cobbett, vol. 1, 54
Parts: Schott 2464
Parts, collections: Breitkopf (with BWV1038, G major);
      Peters (with BWV1038, G minor, sonata, C minor) 237;
      Schirmer

PURCELL   Chacony, 2 vlns, vc, continuo, G minor,
                  "Great." Pub. 1697. 10 min. Easy.

Chacony is an old English word for Chaconne, the
dance in slow triple time. The harmonic basis is a basso
ostinato, just as in a passacaglia. It is a deeply moving
piece in the style of Italian vocal monody. Purcell was the
first in England to reflect the revolution from the old polyphony to the new monody. This is the sixth of ten pieces
in four parts. The cello part could be played by any bass
instrument in Purcell's time.
Parts: Chester; International (Lyman)
Score: Chester

PURCELL   Sonata, 2 vlns, continuo, vc ad. lib., F
                 major, "Golden." Pub. 1697. 10 min.
                 Easy to Int. / Allegro. Adagio. (Can-
                 zona) Allegro. Grave. Allegro.

This is the ninth of ten sonatas for four parts published by Purcell's widow in 1697. According to the Zim-
merman catalog, the name "Golden" first appeared in 1704.
In all of the sonatas a cello may double the keyboard or play
the continuo alone.
Parts: International (Woehl); Schott

TELEMANN   Sonata, 2 vlns, continuo, vc ad. lib., A
                 major. 8 min. Int. / Largo. Vivace.
                 Affettuoso. Allegro.

Telemann was one of the most prolific composers of
the pre-classical period. The trio sonatas have great appeal
and may be played by flute as well as violin. Purchase of
the two-volume set by Schott is recommended.
Parts: International (Lyman)
Parts, collections: Schott 4690/4691 (6 trio sonatas)

CORELLI   Twelve Chamber Sonatas, 2 vlns, continuo,
                 vc/vla da gamba ad. lib., op. 2, D major;
                 D minor; C major; E minor; B flat major;
                 G minor; F major; B minor; F sharp minor;
                 E major; E flat major; G major. 8 min.
                 each. Easy to Int.

All the sonatas are based on the pattern of a suite
with movements of alternating tempi; there is an op. 1 with
12 sonatas also.
Parts: Bärenreiter 701/2/3/4; International; Schott 5430/1/
    2/3

TARTINI   Two Trio Sonatas, 2 vlns, vc, op. 3, no.
                 2, D major; op. 3 no. 4, D major. 4 min.
                 each. Int.

There are many Tartini sonatas available which can be
found in String Music in Print; these are classed as intermediate rather than easy because there are some violin passages in third position.
Parts: Edition Musicus; International

TELEMANN   Sonata, fl, ob, continuo, D minor. Pub.
                 1724. 9 min. Int. / Largo. Allegro.
                 Affettuoso. Presto.

This sonata is from the collection called Essercizi
Musici which contained 12 solo sonatas and 12 trio sonatas.
Also recommended is the sonata from this collection (in E
minor) for recorder, oboe, and continuo. Both sonatas are
similarly constructed; the fast movements of the D minor
are in fugal style.
Parts: Bärenreiter; Breitkopf; Hortus Musicus (Ruetz);
     Schott

TELEMANN   Sonata, ob, harpsichord, continuo, E flat
                major. Pub. 1724. 10 min. Int. /
                Largo. Vivace. Mesto. Vivace.

This sonata, number 12 of the Essercizi Musici is
unusual in that the obbligato part for harpsichord is completely
written out. The righthand part functions as an independent
melodic line interweaving with that of the oboe.
Parts: Sikorski 392

TELEMANN   Concerto a tré, recorder, hn, continuo.
                10 min. Int. to Adv. / Allegro moderato.
                Louré. Tempo di Menuet.

This three-movement work has a most unusual instrumentation; because of this, Telemann contrasts the timbres
rather than combines them. There is a richer bass line
and richer harmonies than in most trio sonatas.
Parts: Hinrichsen

FASCH   Sonata, recorder, ob, vln, continuo, B flat
                major. 10 min. Int. / Largo. Allegro.
                Grave. Allegro.

The use of four voices rather than three is uncommon;
the second movement is a fugue; the oboe part may be played
by violin.
Parts: Nagels Musik-Archiv 148

4 QUARTETS

STRING

*MOZART Quartet, string, K. 387, G major, "Fugue."
1782. Ded. Joseph Haydn. 28 min. Adv.
/ Allegro vivace assai. (Menuetto) Allegro. Andante cantabile. Molto allegro.

Mozart dedicated this and the following five quartets
to Haydn; they are referred to as the "Haydn" quartets. In
his touching dedication he refers to them as his children,
the "fruit of long and laborious endeavor." Just as Haydn's
op. 33 represented a significant step forward in genuine four-
part writing, so these are parallel achievements for Mozart.
It was actually Haydn's op. 33 which inspired Mozart to
undertake a group of six quartets in the "new style." These
quartets are published with K. 499 "Hoffmeister" and K.
575, K. 589, and K. 590 "Prussian Quartets" as the "Celebrated Quartets. "

 Barrett-Ayres, 187-201 Ferguson, 58-59
 Cobbett, vol. 2, 157 King, 19-20
 Dunhill, <u>Mozart</u>, Part Landon, 103-16
  1, 28-35
Parts: Breitkopf; Kalmus; Schirmer L1818
Parts, collections: Bärenreiter 4750; Kalmus; Peters 16;
 Schirmer L1818
Score: Barenreiter TP140 (10 qts); Universal Edition Ph327

*MOZART Quartet, string, K. 417b (421), D minor,
"Eulenspiegel." 1783. Ded. Joseph Haydn.
28 min. Adv. / Allegro moderato. Andante. (Menuetto) Allegretto. Allegretto
ma non troppo.

There are so many beautiful moments in Mozart string
quartets that it is difficult to select highlights. This entire
quartet seems overlaid with pathos. During the second movement there is an arresting shift of tonality toward the middle;

during the Menuetto there is a dramatic moment when the
violin shifts from minor to major, accompanied by simple
pizzicato chords in the other strings.

Cobbett, vol. 2, 157   King, 20-21
Dunhill, Mozart, Part   Landon, 116-19
  1, 35-43
Ferguson, 59-60
Parts: Breitkopf; Novello (Einstein)
Parts, collections: Bärenreiter 4750; Kalmus; Peters 16;
  Schirmer L1818
Score: Bärenreiter TP140 (10 qts); Eulenberg; Universal
  Edition Ph328

*MOZART   Quartet, string, K. 428, E flat major.
                 1783. Ded. Joseph Haydn. 28 min. Adv.
                 / Allegro non troppo. Andante con moto.
                 (Menuetto) Allegro. Allegro vivace.

Strong contrasts from a meditative second movement
to a Finale that is a dance. The Andante, set in 6/8 meter,
proceeds calmly with many rising chromatic passages and
chromatic syncopations, which gives it a "murky" quality.
This is dispelled by the strong rhythmic opening of the Menuetto.

Cobbett, vol. 2, 158   King, 21-22
Dunhill, Mozart, Part   Landon, 122-25
  1, 43-49
Ferguson, 60-61
Parts: Breitkopf; Novello (Einstein)
Parts, collections: Bärenreiter 4750; Kalmus; Peters 16;
  Schirmer L1818
Score: Bärenreiter TP140; Eulenberg; Universal Edition
  Ph329

*MOZART   Quartet, string, K. 458, B flat major,
                 "Hunt." 1784. Ded. Joseph Haydn. 27
                 min. Adv. / Allegro vivace assai. (Men-
                 uetto) Moderato. Adagio. Allegro assai.

The opening bars of the quartet, in 6/8 meter, sound
like the call of the hunting horn; its outer movements are
full of good humor, while the Adagio is a long extended solo
for violin with many florid passages.

Cobbett, vol. 2, 158   King, 25-26
Dunhill, Mozart, Part   Landon, 119-22
  2, 5-11
Ferguson, 61-62
Parts: Breitkopf; Novello (Einstein)

Parts, collections: Bärenreiter 4750; Kalmus; Peters 16;
    Schirmer L1818
Score: Bärenreiter TP140 (10 qts); Eulenberg; Universal
    Edition Ph330

*MOZART   Quartet, string, K. 464, A major, "Drum."
                   1785. Ded. Joseph Haydn. 24 min. Adv.
                   / Allegro. Menuetto. Andante. Allegro.

    This is considered by some to be the most skillfully
crafted of the six "Haydn" quartets. Certainly, the Andante
movement is a marvel of ingenuity, with six variations in
all. The first movement clearly demonstrates Mozart's
genius for combining polyphonic and homophonic techniques.
    Cobbett, vol. 2, 158   King, 26-28
    Dunhill, Mozart, Part   Landon, 125-26
        2, 11-15
    Ferguson, 62-66
Parts: Novello (Einstein)
Parts, collections: Bärenreiter 4750; Kalmus; Peters 16;
    Schirmer L1818
Score: Bärenreiter TP140 (10 qts); Eulenberg; Universal
    Edition Ph331.

*MOZART   Quartet, string, K. 465, C major, "Dis-
                   sonant." 1785. Ded. Joseph Haydn. 28
                   min. Adv. / Adagio-Allegro. Andante
                   cantabile. (Menuetto) Allegro. Allegro
                   molto.

    Tonal ambiguities of the first movement gave rise to
the quartet's name. It is an unusual first movement, beginning with an Adagio. This is a powerful work as evidenced
by the second movement which is especially intense and difficult.
    Cobbett, vol. 2, 158-59   King, 28-31
    Dunhill, Mozart, Part   Landon, 126-30
        2, 16-24
    Ferguson, 62-63
Parts, collections: Bärenreiter 4750; Kalmus; Peters 16;
    Schirmer L1818
Score: Bärenreiter TP140 (10 qts); Eulenberg; Universal
    Edition Ph332

*MOZART   Quartet, string, K. 575, D major, "Prus-
                   sian." 1789. Ded. Friedrich Wilhelm of
                   Prussia. 22 min. Adv. / Allegretto.
                   Andante. (Menuetto) Allegretto. Allegretto.

In the last three quartets, dedicated to the royal amateur, Mozart allows the cello a little more prominence than
usual.   The cello voice is written in a higher range, also.
Although not so significant as the "Haydn" quartets, the
"Prussian" quartets are filled with sophisticated harmonic
surprises.

    Cobbett, vol. 2, 159-60   King, 45-51
    Dunhill, Mozart, Part   Landon, 131-32
      2, 34-37
Parts: Novello (Einstein)
Parts, collections: Bärenreiter 4750; Kalmus; Peters 16;
    Schirmer L1818
Score: Bärenreiter TP140 (10 qts); Eulenberg; Universal Edi-
    tion Ph334

*MOZART   Quartet, string, K. 589, B flat major,
           "Prussian." 1790.   Ded. Friedrich Wilhelm
           of Prussia. 23 min. Adv. / Allegro.
           Larghetto. (Menuetto) Moderato. Allegro
           assai.

The Menuetto is noteworthy--it is quite long, it has
a more complex structure than usual, and its instrumental
passages are florid.   The Finale, though joyful in mood, ends
quietly.

    Cobbett, vol. 2, 160   Landon, 131-32
    Dunhill, Mozart, Part
      2, 38-39
Parts: Novello (Einstein)
Parts, collections: Bärenreiter 4750; Kalmus; Peters 16;
    Schirmer L1818
Score: Bärenreiter TP140 (10 qts); Eulenberg; Universal
    Edition Ph335

*MOZART   Quartet, string, K. 590, F major, "Prus-
           sian." 1790.   Ded. Friedrich Wilhelm of
           Prussia. 25 min. Adv. / Allegro mod-
           erato. (Andante) Allegretto. (Menuetto)
           Allegretto. Allegro.

This quartet generates a great deal of excitement and
propulsion; there are many virtuoso passages, not only for
cello, but for all the parts.   The last movement is filled
with dramatic pauses, which were to become typical Beethoven
effects; some startling shifts of tonality.

    Cobbett, vol. 2, 160   King, 45-51
    Dunhill, Mozart, Part   Landon, 131-32
      2, 39-44

Parts: Novello (Einstein)
Parts, collections: Bärenreiter 4750; Kalmus; Peters 16;
   Schirmer L1818
Score: Bärenreiter TP140; Eulenberg; Universal Edition
   Ph336

*MOZART   Eine kleine Nachtmusik (A Little Night Mu-
       sic), string quartet, K. 525. 1787. 20
       min. Int. / Allegro. (Romance) Andante.
       (Menuetto) Allegretto. (Rondo) Allegro.

  This is heard as a quartet, as a quintet, and as a
piece for chamber orchestra. Every string player seems to
know his part from memory. Hans Keller in his article in
Scherman and Biancolli's Mozart Companion, says that from
the quartet player's standpoint, it is the easiest introduction
to great, perfect Mozart.
  Einstein, Mozart, 206-7
Parts: Peters 3953; Schott 3155
Parts, collections: Peters 17 (17 Easy Quartets)

*HAYDN   Quartet, string, op. 20, no. 4 (Hob. III:34),
       D major. 1772. Ded. Nicolas Zmeskall
       von Domanovetz. 20 min. Adv. / Allegro
       di molto. Un poco Adagio affettuoso.
       (Menuetto) Allegretto alla zingarese. Presto
       scherzando.

  This and the following Haydn quartets have been chosen
as representative of his 83 quartets. Purchase of the complete quartets is recommended as Haydn's quartets are considered the backbone of the string quartet literature. The
Peters editions are popular with string players, and if the
four volumes cannot be purchased at one time, proceed with
volume one and work up to volume four. The more celebrated quartets are in the first two volumes. Opus 20 demonstrates how Haydn first begins to use the four instruments
as equals instead of subordinating the lower strings to the
solo violin. One of the early editions had a rising sun de-
picted on the cover and since that time the six quartets of
this opus have been called the "Sun" quartets. This particular quartet has an arresting second movement, a theme and
variations which is highly charged emotionally. Tovey, in
his Essays and Lectures on Music has an illuminating chapter
on Haydn's chamber music on pages 1-64. Discussion of op.
20 begins on page 40.
  Barrett-Ayres, 84-136   Robertson, 33-35

Cobbett, vol. 1, 534-   Tovey, Essays, 40-64
       38   Ulrich, 185-209
Ferguson, 30-34
Hughes, 156-60
Parts, collections: Peters 289B; International (30 Celebrated);
    Schirmer L1799/1800
Score: Eulenberg

*HAYDN   Quartet, string, op. 33, no. 3 (Hob. III:39),
                   C major, "Bird." 1782. Ded. Grand Duke
                   Paul of Prussia. 24 min. Adv. / Allegro
                   moderato. (Scherzando) Allegretto. Adagio.
                   (Rondo) Presto.

    In op. 33 Haydn continued to refine texture and to
liberate the lower strings from accompanimental roles, although the solo violin still predominates. The grace notes
and trills that appear no doubt led to the nickname. The
six quartets of op. 33 are also known as "Gli scherzi," the
"Maiden" and the "Russian" quartets.
    Barrett-Ayres, 153-70   Hughes, 161
    Cobbett, vol. 1, 538-40   Robertson, 33-35
    Ferguson, 34-35   Ulrich, 185-209
Parts: Breitkopf
Parts, collections: Peters 289B; International (30 Cele-
    brated); Schirmer L1799/1800

*HAYDN   Quartet, string, op. 50, no. 1 (Hob. III:44),
                   B flat major. 1787. Ded. Friedrich Wil-
                   helm II of Prussia. 22 min. Adv. /
                   Allegro. Adagio non lento. (Menuetto)
                   Poco allegretto. (Finale) Vivace.

    This is an example of a very inventive quartet which
is neglected, and yet every time it is played, it elicits much
enthusiasm. Haydn is very economical here--he builds entire
movements out of a few motifs. In all of the movements
the strings share equally in the development of the thematic
material. The last movement is a rapid-fire one, with many
dramatic pauses and many fugal entries. The solo violin has
a short cadenza.
    Barrett-Ayres, 202-11   Ulrich, 185-209
    Cobbett, vol. 1, 543-44
Parts, collections: Peters 289C
Score: Eulenberg

*HAYDN   Quartet, string, op. 64, no. 5 (Hob. III:67),

D major, "Lark." 1790. Comm. Johann
Tost. 21 min. Adv. / Allegro moderato.
Adagio cantabile. (Menuetto) Allegretto.
(Finale) Vivace.

This is one of the most popular quartets--it represents
Haydn at his best, with many harmonic surprises and great
contrapuntal skill in evidence. The last movement is a perpetual motion employing staccato sixteenth notes. There are
six quartets in op. 64.

Barrett-Ayres, 246-63   Robertson, 39-41
Cobbett, vol. 1, 544   Ulrich, 185-209
Ferguson, 36-38
Parts, collections: Peters 289B
Score: Boosey; Heugel; Universal

*HAYDN   Quartet, string, op. 76, no. 2 (Hob. III:76),
                D minor, "Quinten." 1797. Ded. Count
                Erdödy. 20 min. Adv. / Allegro. An-
                dante o più tosto allegretto. (Menuetto)
                Allegro ma non troppo. (Finale) Vivace
                assai.

This is the only quartet of the six in this opus which
is in the minor mode; in the second movement Haydn alternates between major and minor. The first movement is
built on melodic intervals at the fifth, hence the name "Quin-
ten." The third movement is a very unusual Minuet, called
the "Witches Minuet" because of the very close canon in
octaves between pairs of instruments; the Trio section is in
a completely different style, a homophonic dance.

Barrett-Ayres, 297-312   Robertson, 45-52
Cobbett, vol. 1, 545   Ulrich, 185-209
Parts: Augener; Breitkopf
Parts, collections: International (30 Celebrated); Kalmus;
     Peters 289B (16 Famous); Schirmer 1799/1800
Score: Boosey; Eulenberg; Heugel; Universal Edition

*HAYDN   Quartet, string, op. 76, no. 3 (Hob. III:77),
                C major, "Kaiser." 1797. Ded. Count
                Erdödy. 27 min. Adv. / Allegro. Poco
                adagio, cantabile. (Menuetto) Allegro. (Fi-
                nale) Presto.

The second movement is a sublime set of variations
on the hymn which Haydn wrote to celebrate the birthday of
the emperor of Austria. The hymn itself is one of the most
beautiful in existence. It was adopted by the Nazi regime

with the text "Deutschland über Alles" and consequently, this lovely quartet was not heard in concert halls for many years. Haydn gives the statement of the hymn to each person in the quartet and weaves four variations around it. The first movement is typical of Haydn's monothematic approach, in which he develops motifs in as many different ways as possible with the same motif or motifs serving throughout the movement.

Barrett-Ayres, 297-312   Robertson, 45-52
Cobbett, vol. 1, 545   Ulrich, 185-209
Parts: Peters 288
Parts, collections: International (30 Celebrated); Peters 289B
Score: Boosey; Eulenberg; Heugel; Universal Edition

*BEETHOVEN   Quartet, string, op. 18, no. 1, F major. 1799-1801. Ded. Prince Lobkowitz. 26 min. Adv. / Allegro con brio. Adagio affettuoso ed appassionato. (Scherzo) Allegro molto. Allegro.

Opus 18 is the culmination of Beethoven's early period. Unique as the quartets are, they are modeled on the quartets of Haydn and Mozart. These and later quartets show Beethoven as a master architect, developing and transforming motifs innumerable ways, and as a master dramatist, with sudden changes of dynamics, unexpected accents and surprise modulations. Also, in these quartets, there is great independence of the parts. The numbering does not reflect the order in which they were written; the first, considered by some to be the most difficult, was not the first one written. Its first movement is notable for the exhaustive treatment of its opening motif; the second movement for its beautifully expressive dual themes, one in minor, the other in major.

Cobbett, vol. 1, 106-7   Marliave, 4-12
Ferguson, 95-96   Mason, Beethoven, 15-30
Hadow, 14-22   Radcliffe, Beethoven, 22-
Kerman, 30-44   47 (op. 18)
Lam, Part 1, 12-18   Robertson, 110-16 (op. 18)
Scherman, 207-11
Parts: Breitkopf; Kalmus; Schirmer
Parts, collections: Henle 139; Kalmus; Peters 195A; Schirmer L1808
Score: Boosey 123; Eulenberg; Lea (17 qts) 61/2/3/4; Universal Edition Ph310

*BEETHOVEN   Quartet, string, op. 18, no. 2, G major,

"Compliments." 1798-1801. Ded. Prince
Lobkowitz. 21 min. Adv. / Allegro.
Adagio cantabile. (Scherzo) Allegro. Al-
legro molto quasi presto.

The entire first movement is built on three short motifs that are presented within the first six measures. The
slow movement is unique in that after 26 or so bars, a
dance theme appears with an abrupt change of key, meter,
and tempo--the movement closes with a return of the Adagio
in the original key. The first violin part here is florid and
soloistic. The last two movements are full of good humor.

Cobbett, vol. 1, 108   Marliave, 12-17
Ferguson, 96   Mason, Beethoven, 31-40
Hadow, Part 1, 23-31   Radcliffe, Beethoven, 22-
Kerman, 44-53   47 (op. 18)
Lam, Part 1, 18-22   Robertson, 110-16 (op. 18)
                               Scherman, 211-13
Parts: Breitkopf; Kalmus; Schirmer
Parts, collections: Henle 139; Kalmus; Peters 195A; Schir-
  mer L1808
Score: Boosey 124; Eulenberg; Lea (17 qts) 61/2/3/4;
  Universal Edition Ph311

*BEETHOVEN   Quartet, string, op. 18, no. 3, D major.
              1798-1801. Ded. Prince Lobkowitz. 24
              min. Adv. / Allegro. Andante con
              moto. Allegro. Presto.

This is a good introduction to op. 18--it was probably
the first one composed. The opening motif, a rising seventh
interval, is passed from voice to voice. The entire first
movement is dramatic. The third movement has charming
pauses scattered throughout; the fourth is a swift dance in
6/8 meter.

Cobbett, vol. 1, 87,   Marliave, 17-22
  108   Mason, Beethoven, 41-48
Ferguson, 97   Radcliffe, Beethoven, 22-
Hadow, 31-40   47 (op. 18)
Kerman, 10-25   Robertson, 110-16 (op.
Lam, Part 1, 22-24   18)
                               Scherman, 213-14
Parts: Breitkopf; Kalmus; Schirmer
Parts, collections: Henle 139; Kalmus; Peters 195A; Schir-
  mer L1808
Score: Boosey 125; Eulenberg; Universal Edition Ph312

*BEETHOVEN   Quartet, string, op. 18, no. 4, C minor.

1798-1801. Ded. Prince Lobkowitz. 23
min. Adv. / Allegro ma non tanto.
(Scherzo) Andante scherzoso quasi allegretto.
(Menuetto) Allegretto. Allegro-Prestissimo.

This quartet is special, the tonality indicative of its
significance, C minor reserved for Beethoven's weightier
moments. The second movement, instead of being the usual
Adagio, is a tightly-knit Scherzo in fugal style.

Cobbett, vol. 1, 108   Marliave, 22-31
Ferguson, 97-98   Mason, Beethoven, 49-55
Hadow, 40-48   Radcliffe, Beethoven, 22-
Kerman, 82-90   47 (op. 18)
Lam, Part 1, 24-27   Robertson, 110-16 (op.
    18)
    Scherman, 214-16

Parts: Breitkopf; Kalmus; Schirmer
Parts, collections: Henle 139; Kalmus; Peters 195A; Schirmer L1808
Score: Boosey 126; Eulenberg; Universal Edition Ph313

*BEETHOVEN   Quartet, string, op. 18, no. 5, A major.
1798-1801. Ded. Prince Lobkowitz. 24
min. Adv. / Allegro. Menuetto. Andante cantabile. Allegro.

This quartet is Mozartean in style throughout. The
Andante is an unusual set of extended variations with a mischievous turn at the coda.

Cobbett, vol. 1, 108   Marliave, 31-40
Ferguson, 99   Mason, Beethoven, 56-69
Hadow, 48-54   Radcliffe, Beethoven, 22-
Kerman, 55-65   47 (op. 18)
Lam, Part 1, 28-31   Robertson, 110-16 (op.
    18)
    Scherman, 216-21

Parts: Breitkopf; Kalmus; Schirmer
Parts, collections: Henle 139; Kalmus; Peters 195A; Schirmer L1808
Score: Boosey 127; Eulenberg; Universal Edition Ph314

*BEETHOVEN   Quartet, string, op. 18, no. 6, B flat major.
1798-1801. Ded. Prince Lobkowitz. 25
min. Adv. / Allegro con brio. Adagio
ma non troppo. (Scherzo) Allegro molto.
(La Malinconia, Questo pezzo si deve trattare colla più gran delicatezza) Adagio-Allegretto quasi allegro.

The beginning movement looks backward to Haydn and Mozart; the last movement is dramatically different. The Adagio theme "La Malinconia" is interrupted three times by a gay Allegretto each time it tries to reassert itself, but the Allegretto theme "wins out" and becomes a Prestissimo at the end. The Scherzo movement is filled with sudden accents and syncopations which deceive the ear at every turn! The second movement theme is beautifully embellished.

Ferguson, 99-100   Mason, Beethoven, 70-79
Hadow, 54-63   Radcliffe, Beethoven, 22-
Kerman, 65-82; 75-81   47
Lam, Part 1, 31-33   Robertson, 110-16 (op.
Marliave, 40-50   18)
                          Scherman, 221-27

Parts: Breitkopf; Kalmus; Schirmer
Parts, collections: Henle 139; Kalmus; Peters 195A; Schirmer L1808
Score: Boosey 128; Eulenberg; Universal Edition Ph315

*BEETHOVEN   Quartet, string, op. 59, no. 1, F major, "Rasumovsky." 1806. Ded. Count Rasumovsky. 42 min. Adv. / Allegro. Allegretto vivace e sempre scherzando. Adagio molto e mesto. (Thème russe) Allegro.

The three works of op. 59 represent the composer's middle period and are consequently more complex, with less looking back to Haydn and Mozart. Count Rasumovsky was the Russian ambassador to Vienna who had a great appreciation of the arts and who also played the violin. In this first quartet the majority of the movements are cast in the sonata-allegro mold, including the Scherzo, which is also unusually long and in a unique position of following the first movement. It begins with a drumming effect in the cello part which continues throughout the movement in one part or another. The coda is a breathtaking one in fugal style. The Adagio, full of pathos heightened by pizzicato, ends with a violin cadenza which becomes the transition to the Finale. The Finale itself is based on a Russian tune. Most of the editions of op. 59 also include op. 74 and op. 95.

Abraham, 13-28   Marliave, 62-89
Cobbett, vol. 1, 93-95   Mason, Beethoven, 83-
Ferguson, 100-104   101
Kerman, 151-54; 93-   Radcliffe, Beethoven, 48-
  116   81
Lam, Part 1, 36-50   Robertson, 118-22
                          Scherman, 695-715

Parts: Breitkopf

Parts, collections: Kalmus; Peters 195B; Schirmer L1809
Score: Boosey 129; Eulenberg; Universal Edition Ph316

*BEETHOVEN   Quartet, string, op. 59, no. 2, E minor,
              "Rasoumovsky." 1806. Ded. Count Rasu-
              movsky. 28 min. Adv. / Allegro.
              Molto adagio, si tratta questo pezzo con
              molto di sentimento. Allegretto. Presto.

        Simpler and less dramatic than op. 59, no. 1, but
with just as much harmonic and thematic integration. The
Russian "tune" appears here in the Trio section of the Scherzo
where the major mode is used to contrast with the minor
opening. Attention is usually called to the opening of the
Presto, where the tonal center is ambiguous; C major and
E minor alternate, with the latter ultimately dominating.

Abraham, 28-41   Marliave, 89-115
Cobbett, vol. 1, 95   Mason, Beethoven, 102-
Ferguson, 104-5   15
Kerman, 51-54; 120-   Radcliffe, Beethoven,
  34   48-81
Lam, Part 1, 51-57   Robertson, 122-24
                                 Scherman, 715-17

Parts: Breitkopf
Parts, collections: Kalmus; Peters 195B; Schirmer L1809
Score: Boosey 130; Eulenberg; Universal Edition Ph317

*BEETHOVEN   Quartet, string, op. 59, no. 3, C major,
              "Rasoumovsky." 1806. Ded. Count Rasu-
              movsky. 30 min. Adv. / (Introduzione)
              Andante con moto-Allegro vivace. Andante
              con moto quasi allegretto. (Menuetto) Gra-
              zioso. Allegro molto.

        The third quartet of op. 59, which was the most ac-
ceptable to Beethoven's contemporaries, is considered by
some critics since to be inferior to the other two; however,
critics and performers alike find the last movement fugue
a breathtaking experience. Some of the more unusual aspects
of this quartet are the slow, mysterious introduction to the
first movement with its ambiguous tonality, the pizzicato
cello effects in the meditative slow movement, the charming
pauses scattered throughout the Menuetto and the swift, dance-
like Finale in 6/8 meter.

Abraham, 41-54   Marliave, 116-47
Cobbett, vol. 1, 95-   Mason, Beethoven, 116-
  96   27
Ferguson, 105-7   Radcliffe, Beethoven, 48-
                                  81

Kerman, 151-54;   Robertson, 124-25
    134-50   Scherman, 718-26
Lam, Part 1, 58-64
Parts: Breitkopf
Parts, collections: Kalmus; Peters 195B; Schirmer L1809
Score: Boosey 131; Eulenberg; Universal Edition Ph318

BEETHOVEN   Quartet, string, op. 74, E flat major,
              "Harp." 1809. Ded. Joseph von Lobkowitz.
              32 min. Adv. / Poco Adagio-Allegro.
              Adagio, ma non troppo. Presto. Allegretto
              con variazioni.

    Like the preceding quartet, op. 74 opens with an
Adagio introduction to an Allegro. The pizzicato effects in
the first movement sound like a harp; hence, the nickname.
Basil Lam describes the quartet as "a 'poco adagio' introduction, full of elevated sentiment like the best Schumann, a
brilliantly scored quasi-symphonic 'Allegro', a lyrical, richly
elaborated 'adagio', a laconic scherzo alternating with a trio
in deliberately rough polyphony and, for conclusion, a neatly
trimmed set of variations on a good-humoured theme."
    Abraham, 54-67   Marliave, 147-73
    Cobbett, vol. 1, 96-97   Mason, Beethoven, 128-44
    Ferguson, 107-8   Radcliffe, Beethoven, 82-
    Kerman, 156-68   89
    Lam, Part 1, 64-68   Robertson, 125
                               Scherman, 726-34
Parts, collections: Kalmus; Peters 195B; Schirmer L1809
Score: Bärenreiter; Boosey 132; Eulenberg; Universal Edi-
    tion Ph319

BEETHOVEN   Quartet, string, op. 95, F minor, "Serioso."
              1810. Ded. N. Zmeskall of Domanowetz.
              23 min. Adv. / Allegro con brio. Al-
              legretto ma non troppo. Larghetto espres-
              sivo-Allegretto agitato-Allegro.

    This is transitional between Beethoven's middle and
late periods; it anticipates characteristics of the late, including compression of ideas, abrupt conjunctions of themes,
and the breaking down of the traditional sonata and rondo
forms. The second movement is unorthodox with its tonality
unrelated to that of the first; the epilogue of the Presto is
equally unorthodox, its tonality F major instead of F minor.
    Abraham, 67-79   Marliave, 173-96
    Cobbett, vol. 1, 97-99   Mason, Beethoven, 145-
                                  59

Ferguson, 108-11   Radcliffe, <u>Beethoven</u>,
Kerman, 168-87   89-98
Lam, Part 2, 5-11   Robertson, 125-26
                           Scherman, 734-46
Parts, collections: Kalmus; Peters 195B; Schirmer L1809
Score: Boosey 133; Eulenberg; Universal Edition Ph320

*SCHUBERT   Quartet, string, op. 29, no. 1 (D. 804),
                 A minor. Pub. 1824. Ded. Ignaz Schup-
                 panzigh. 33 min. Adv. / Allegro ma
                 non troppo. Andante. (Menuetto) Allegretto.
                 Allegro moderato.

One of the most poignant quartets in the literature,
especially the Menuetto; some characteristics that are typical
of Schubert are the accompaniment patterns that are highly
chromatic, the strong emphasis on melody, with the first
violin assuming the lead, the sudden shifts in tonality and
meter. Although the Schubert quartets are available as separates, purchase of the complete quartets in two volumes
(Peters) is recommended.

Cobbett, vol. 2, 358-   Ferguson, 143-44
   59   Robertson, 158-59
Coolidge, 309-25   Westrup, 30-35
Einstein, <u>Schubert</u>,
   252-53
Parts: Breitkopf; Universal Edition 88
Parts, collections: Peters 168A/B (9 qts; D. 804 in 168A)
Score: Boosey 186; Eulenberg (Peters E40); Universal Edi-
   tion Ph351.

*SCHUBERT   Quartet, string, op. posth. (D. 810), D.
                 minor, "Death and the Maiden." 1824-26.
                 36 min. Adv. / Allegro. Andante con
                 moto. (Scherzo) Allegro molto. Presto.

The first movement is intense and tightly organized;
the second, a theme and variations based on Schubert's song
"Der Tod und das Mädchen," begins and ends with a presentation
of the theme in a hymn setting. The Scherzo is agitated, and
in spite of a calmer Trio section in the contrasting major mode,
the agitation continues just under the surface; the Presto is an
aggravated Tarentella with a breathless ending.

Brent-Smith, 5-29   Ferguson, 144-46
Cobbett, vol. 2, 359-   Robertson, 159-60
   60   Westrup, 35-42
Coolidge, 309-25
Einstein, <u>Schubert</u>, 254-
   56

Parts: Breitkopf
Parts, collections: Peters 168A/B (9 qts; D. 810 in 168A)
Score: Boosey 188; Eulenberg (Peters E11); Universal Edition Ph352

*SCHUBERT   Quartet, string, D. 703, C minor, "Quartet-
             tsatz." Pub. 1870. 8 min. Adv. /
             Allegro assai.

It is conjectured that Schubert planned this as a first
movement to a quartet, but no traces of other movements
have been found. This brief piece is evidence enough that
Schubert was coming into a new style, moving away from
Beethoven influence. The 6/8 meter is unusual for an opening movement; it is very intense and frenzied, without the
transparency associated with Schubert. Another single movement in the same key which is a manuscript fragment that
was reconstructed might be confused with this movement--
it dates from an earlier period (D. 103) and is suitable for
intermediate level.

Cobbett, vol. 2, 357   Ferguson, 142-43
Coolidge, 309-25   Robertson, 158
Einstein, Schubert,   Westrup, 28-30
   160-61
Parts, collections: Peters 168B
Score: Eulenberg (Peters E354); Universal Edition Ph350

SCHUBERT   Quartet, string, op. 161 (D. 887), G major.
             1826. 42 min. Adv. / Allegro molto
             moderato. Andante un poco moto. (Scherzo)
             Allegro vivace. Allegro assai.

With his last quartet Schubert moves away from extended song as a unifying factor toward a more fragmentary
thematic style; some themes appear in a chromatic fabric;
accompanying parts are limited to chordal patterns rather
than interplay; throughout the work there are frequent passages of tremolo and repeated note patterns, frequent harmonic shifts to adjacent keys, and dramatic outbursts, especially in the second movement. The outer movements
vacillate between major and minor. The first two movements
are quite weighty--the last two have been criticized as lacking in organic relationship to the first two.

Cobbett, vol. 2, 360-   Truscott, Schubert, 119-
   62   45
Coolidge, 309-25   Westrup, 42-46
Ferguson, 146-49

Parts: Breitkopf
Parts, collections: Peters 168B
Score: Boosey 187; Eulenberg (Peters E39); Universal Edition Ph353

*DVOŘÁK   Quartet, string, op. 96 (B. 179), F major,
               "American." 1893. 24 min. Adv. /
               Allegro ma non troppo. Lento. Molto
               vivace. (Finale) Vivace ma non troppo.

    This is one of the most popular quartets in the literature; the first movement opens with a broad theme introduced by the cello and passed from one instrument to another during the exposition. Dvořák's melodies and rhythms are partly imitative of American Indian melodies and rhythms and partly Slavic in character. A listener would identify this immediately with the composer of the "New World" symphony. It is a thickly textured work, even in the lighter third movement. The Finale is full of climaxes of sound, which can be taxing to the players and problematic for intonation.
    Cobbett, vol. 1, 360-   Sourek, 96-104
        62
    Ferguson, 234-35
Parts: Artia; International; Simrock
Score: Artia; Eulenberg (Peters E302); International

*DEBUSSY   Quartet, string, op. 10, G minor. 1893.
               25 min. Adv. / Animé et très décidé.
               Assez vif et bien rhythmé. Andantino,
               doucement expressif. Très modéré.

    Debussy has based the thematic development of the entire quartet on a germinal motif which appears in the opening two measures; sometimes its subsequent appearances are obvious, sometimes they are disguised. Even though the harmonies are quite chromatic, the listener feels that key centers are firmly established. Debussy was an innovator in a harmonic and textural sense. Throughout there are special effects created by muted strings, pizzicato and arco combinations, and tremolo. Murmuring effects appear frequently which are created by the use of triplets and a rocking back and forth on intervals of a second or a third. Especially effective is the opening of the second movement where the viola plays an arco solo against a pizzicato background. Also effective is the ethereal opening and close of the third. Key signatures of four, five, or six sharps or flats may prove troublesome to the players and there are

some difficult double stops, with many passages of octaves
for the first violin.

Cobbett, vol. 1, 317- Ferguson, 257-59
18
Parts: Durand; International; Kalmus
Score: Durand; International; Peters E210

DVOŘÁK   Quartet, string, op. 51 (B. 92), E flat
              major. 1878-79. Ded. Jean Becker. 32
              min. Adv. / Allegro ma non troppo.
              (Dumka) Elegia, Andante con moto-Vivace.
              (Romanze) Andante con moto. (Finale)
              Allegro assai.

A very ingratiating, exuberant work, with many Slavic
melodies; the second movement is based on the dumka and
has the alternating melancholy and gaiety found in that folk
form; a good introduction to Dvořák because the parts are
more manageable than those of either op. 105 or op. 96.

Cobbett, vol. 1, 358- Sourek, 83-88
59
Ferguson, 233-34
Parts: Artia; International; Simrock
Score: Artia; Eulenberg (Peters E299)

DVOŘÁK   Quartet, string, op. 105 (B. 193), A flat
              major. 1895. 32 min. Adv. / Adagio
              ma non troppo. Allegro appassionata.
              Molto vivace. Lento e molto cantabile.
              Allegro non tanto.

An extraordinary quartet, not heard often; it is not
the "New World" Dvořák or the folk music Dvořák but rather
a distillation, musically, that reaches to a higher artistic
level; there are many chromatic passages and dynamic contrasts; the texture varies quite often with many solo passages.
The Lento is mysterious and dark; the Scherzo, lilting.

Cobbett, vol. 1, 363- Sourek, 104-12
64
Parts: Artia; International; Simrock
Score: Artia; Eulenberg (Peters E303)

BRAHMS   Quartet, string, op. 51, no. 2, A minor.
              Pub. 1873. Ded. Dr. Theodor Billroth.
              32 min. Adv. / Allegro non troppo.
              Andante moderato. (Quasi menuetto) Mod-
              erato, Allegretto vivace. (Finale) Allegro
              non assai.

Brahms' two quartets of op. 51 (C minor, A minor)
and op. 67 in B flat major show his mastery of the form.
He was supposed to have destroyed many before these were
published.   Even though they are difficult for the amateur,
purchase of the three in the Peters edition is recommended.
Op. 51, no. 2 presents fewer hurdles to the players.   It is
lighter in texture and more lyrical than the first.   Throughout, Brahms' subtle and ingenious rhythmic phrasing is evident.   In the second movement, where the parts are soloistic,
especially the cello, there is an antiphonal interplay.   The
Menuetto is filled with longing, its opening melancholy contrasting with recurring bustling episodes.

Cobbett, vol. 1, 173-74	Ferguson, 204-7 (3 qts)
	Keys, 33-39 (3 qts)
Colles, 31-36	Mason, Brahms 97-107
Drinker, 96-97	(op. 51)
Evans, vol. 1, 222-40	

Parts: Breitkopf; International
Parts, collections: Kalmus; Peters 3903 (3 qts)
Score: Boosey HPS219/20/21; Peters 240/41/42

RAVEL   Quartet, string, F major. 1902-3. Ded.
                 Gabriel Fauré. 25 min. Adv. / Allegro
                 moderato-Très doux. Assez vif-Très
                 rythmé. Très lent. Vif et agité.

However unorthodox the chromatic harmonies may
seem, the structure is traditional; the first movement is in
sonata-allegro form and a cyclical theme appears in all movements.   Ravel expands the color resources of the quartet
through devices such as long muted passages, combinations
of pizzicato and arco in unusual ways and use of the bows
near the fingerboard.

Cobbett, vol. 2, 270-71	Ferguson, 260-62
	Myers, 180-81
Demuth, 123-32	

Parts: Durand; International
Score: Durand; International

BARTÓK   Quartet, string, no. 1, op. 7. Pub. 1909.
                 30 min. Adv. / Lento. Allegretto.
                 (Introduzione) Allegro. Allegro vivace.

Bartók's six string quartets are undeniable masterpieces.   The first two, even with complex harmonies and
ambiguous tonalities are more accessible to the player and

listener than the later ones. Recommended order of purchase:
Quartets 1 and 2; 5 and 6; 3 and 4. The first, a highly
charged and dramatic work, begins on a contemplative note
with slow contrapuntal weaving and ends with a finale per-
meated with the folk elements Bartók was beginning to utilize from his pioneer study of Eastern European peasant music. Devices are present which later became recognized as
typical--the frequent unison/octave passages, the long sections of rapid repeated notes, the pedal points, motifs used
as ostinati, and movements linked motivically. The first
movement of the first quartet segues into the second by
means of an accelerating passage and the third, by means of
a concerted cadenza, serves as an introduction to the finale.

> Cobbett, vol. 1, 60-61   Króo, 45-50
> Cohn, Europe, 28-29   Stevens, 170-76
> Ferguson, 273-76

Parts: Boosey; International
Score: Boosey; International; Universal Edition

BARTÓK   Quartet, string, no. 2, op. 17.
                  1915-17. Ded. Hungarian Quartet. 30 min.
                  Adv. + / Moderato. Allegro molto capric-
                  cioso. Lento.

The folk element is more obvious than in the first
quartet. Bartók juxtaposes tonalities, uses modal scales,
drone-like passages of repeated notes, and coloristic harmonizations of what is essentially linear or horizontal writing. A striking aspect is the replacing of movement themes
by a few motifs which are developed throughout the entire
work. The arch form is apparent in the reflective outer
movements surrounding a vigorous dance-like middle movement. This quartet was the first to be recorded (1925) and
was recorded ten years before the first quartet.

> Cobbett, vol. 1, 61-63   Króo, 91-96
> Cohn, Europe, 28, 29   Stevens, 176-83
> Ferguson, 276-79

Parts: Boosey; Universal Edition
Score: Boosey; Universal Edition Ph202

GRIEG   Quartet, string, op. 27, G minor. 1877-78.
                  34 min. Adv. / Un poco Andante-Allegro
                  molto. (Romanze) Andantino. (Intermezzo)
                  Allegro molto marcato. (Finale) Lento-
                  Presto al saltarello.

In spite of being structurally weak, Grieg's assemblage
of melodic ideas has kept this romantic work in the literature

and can provide a stimulating change for players because of
its unusual, unrepresentative structure. It is mostly homophonic in style. The first movement is built on repetitions
of a motto theme first heard in the introduction. The second
movement alternates a romantic song (which each instrument
has an opportunity to present) with agitated episodes. The
third is an intermezzo in the minor mode, but which has a
sprightly, gay quality--it has a rustic dance rhythm accenting the third beat of a 3/4 meter. The last movement, after
a Lento introduction, is rapid and light.
      Cobbett, vol. 1, 498   Frank, 32-44
      Ferguson, 239-40
Parts: Kalmus; Peters 2489
Score: Eulenberg (Peters E276)

FRANCK   Quartet, string, D major. 1889-90. 45
                  min. Adv. / Poco lento. (Scherzo)
                  Vivace. Larghetto. (Final) Allegro molto.

      The quartet, though no longer popular, is an architec-
tural marvel of cyclic form--the first theme heard is the
germinal one, presented in a long slow introduction. The
last movement is composed of alternating slow and fast sections, recalling themes heard earlier. The texture is thick,
the harmonies chromatic, keeping string players taxed to the
limit.
      Cobbett, vol. 1, 426-   Robertson, 246-49
      28
      Ferguson, 368-69
Parts: Hamelle; Peters 3746
Score: Eulenberg (Peters E323); Hamelle

BORODIN   Quartet, string, no. 2, D major. 1880.
                  28 min. Adv. / Allegro moderato.
                  (Scherzo) Allegro. (Notturno) Andante.
                  (Finale) Andante.

      The two inner movements have achieved fame on their
own.   The theme of the second movement has been popular-
ized in the show Kismet, based on Borodin's music.   The
third, Notturno, is exquisite; unfortunately, it has suffered
from overexposure.   The popular theme is linked to an impassioned secondary theme by rushing, ascending scales.
The last is structured a bit differently--the short recitative-
like theme is stated periodically within an Andante tempo and
then treated contrapuntally within a Vivace tempo.
      Cobbett, vol. 1, 151-   Robertson, 415-19
      52
      Ferguson, 220-22

Parts: Breitkopf; International; Peters
Score: Eulenberg (Peters E201); International

SMETANA   Quartet, string, no. 1, E minor, "From
                 My Life." 1876. 30 min. Adv. / Al-
                 legro vivo appassionato. Allegro moderato
                 a la polka. Largo sostenuto. Vivace.

    Smetana himself has written a detailed description of
this autobiographical work. The first movement depicts his
youthful yearnings; the second, his gay life as a youth; the
third, bliss of his love for the girl he later married; and
the fourth, the joy of treating the music of his homeland in
his compositions. In the first movement the theme introduced
by the viola hints of later tragedy and in the final movement
the high, sustained pitch of E signifies the high pitch heard
by the composer as his deafness approached.
        Cobbett, vol. 2, 427-   Robertson, 204-6
          30
        Ferguson, 226
Parts: Artia; Breitkopf; International; Peters 2635
Score: Artia; Eulenberg (Peters E275)

TCHAIKOVSKY   Quartet, string, op. 11, D major. 1871.
              25 min. Adv. / Moderato e semplice.
              Andante cantabile. (Scherzo) Allegro ma non
              tanto. (Finale) Allegro giusto.

    The texture is orchestral and the melodic figurations
familiar to string players who have performed the symphonies.
The second movement has two beautiful themes, one of which
is the famous Andante Cantabile, arranged innumerable times
for a variety of instrumental combinations.
        Cobbett, vol. 2, 491-   Robertson, 411-15
          93
        Ferguson, 222-23
Parts: International; Peters 3172A
Score: Eulenberg (Peters E161)

SCHUMANN   Quartet, string, op. 41, no. 3, A major.
              Pub. 1849. Ded. F. Mendelssohn. 31 min.
              Adv. / Andante espressivo-Allegro molto
              moderato. Assai agitato. Adagio molto.
              (Finale) Allegro molto vivace.

    The first movement is improvisatory in feel, with the
violin or cello usually taking the lead; the second movement

is a unique Scherzo with variations; the last movement has
enormous vitality. Most of Schumann's writing, whether for
string quartet or orchestra is said to be pianistic. Whether
that is so or not, this quartet deserves a place in the standard literature. A good performance will dispel notions of
"pianistic. " It is suggested that the library purchase the
collection of three quartets in op. 41.
     Cobbett, vol. 2, 376-   Page, 88-89
       78
     Ferguson, 171-74
Parts: Breitkopf
Parts, collections: International; Kalmus; Peters 2379
Score: Eulenberg (Peters E74/75/76) (3 qts); Ricordi Pr534/
     35/422 (3 qts)

MENDELSSOHN   Quartet, string, op. 12, E flat major.
                  Pub. 1830. 26 min. Int. / Adagio
                  non troppo. Allegro non tardente. Can-
                  zonetta-Allegretto. Andante espressivo.
                  Molto allegro e vivace.

     This quartet opens and closes on a tranquil note; its
themes are broad and the second movement has all the delicacy we associate with Mendelssohn; it has a folk character
made more distinctive by the "scampering" pizzicato and
staccato effects. String players tend to be disdainful of
Mendelssohn's quartets, but they are accessible to intermediate level players. This opus is not published as a separate
--it is recommended that the editions containing this and the
three quartets of Op. 44 be purchased.
     Cobbett, vol. 2, 131-   Horton, 34-47
       32
     Ferguson, 158-60
Parts, collections: Henle 270; International (4 qts); Kalmus
     (4 qts); Peters 1742
Score: Eulenberg; Lea 149/50 (7 qts)

MOZART   Divertimenti, string quartet, K. 125a(136),
             D major; K. 125b(137), B flat major; K.
             125c(138), F major. 1772. 8 to 10 min.
             each. Easy.

     These early three-movement divertimenti, usually
heard in orchestral versions, are excellent training repertoire
for the neophyte ensemble. Einstein contends that Mozart
was not responsible for designating them as divertimenti and
that, considering their symphonic character, they were probably written as sketches for future symphonies.

Einstein, <u>Mozart</u>, 172-
     73
Parts: Breitkopf (K. 125a; K. 125b)
Parts, collections: International; Kalmus; Peters 4266
Score: Peters 4266A

CLARKE   String Music of the Baroque Era. 2 to 5
                min. each. Easy.

The composers represented in this tasteful collection
of short, easy pieces for string quartet selected, arranged,
and edited by Irma Clarke are Corelli, Rameau, Handel,
J. S. Bach, Purcell, and Telemann. There are many such
collections as this listed under appropriate instrumentations
in the Farish <u>String Music in Print</u>.
Parts: Boston Music Company
Score: Boston Music Company

HINDEMITH   Eight Pieces in the First Position, string
                quartet, op. 44, no. 3. Pub. 1927. 2 to
                3 min. each. Int.

Part of Hindemith's Schulwerk series; first rate material for those moderately advanced in first position; may
be played as a quintet with double bass or as a piece for
string choir.
     Cohn, <u>Europe</u>, 97
Parts: Associated Music Publishers; Schott
Score: Associated Music Publishers; Schott

HOLST   St. Paul's Suite, string quartet, op. 29, no.
                2. 1913. 18 min. Int. / (Jig) Vivace.
                (Ostinato) Presto. (Intermezzo) Andante con
                moto. (Finale, The Dargason) Allegro.

This was not written as chamber music but makes a
worthwhile and enjoyable quartet/quintet for an intermediate
level group; double bass part ad lib. Holst frequently utilizes
folk tunes of the British Isles.
     Cohn, <u>Europe</u>, 121
Parts: Curwen

LOCKE   Consort of Four Parts, string quartet, suite
                no. 1, D minor; no. 2, D major; no. 3, F
                major; no. 4, F major; no. 5, G minor;
                no. 6, G major. 6 to 10 min. each. Easy.

Excellent introductory literature, originally written for

a consort of viols; brief, four-movement dance suites with movements labeled Fantazie, Courante, Ayre, and Saraband. The Stainer & Bell edition, available since 1972, was selected from Musica Brittanica, vol. 32.
> Cobbett, vol. 2, 100-
>   101
Parts: Stainer & Bell (Tilmouth); Peters 6175
Score: Stainer & Bell (Chamber Music of M. Locke, vol. 2.)

SHOSTAKOVICH   Quartet, string, no. 1, op. 49, C major.
                 1938. 16 min. Adv. / Moderato.
                 Moderato. Allegro molto. Allegro.

Simple in concept, lyrical, and in a romantic vein; during the first movement, the cellist has a glissando or two; the second movement, a theme and variations, gives the viola prominence--the viola part is a fortuitous one. The Scherzo is muted and very fast, with a highly contrasted middle section. Shostakovich has written over a dozen quartets which effectively show his development.
> Cobbett, vol. 3, 143-   Martynov, 73-78
>   44
Parts: International; Kalmus
Score: Eulenberg (Peters E385); International

TURINA   La Oración del Torero, op. 34.   10 min.
                 Adv. / Allegro moderato.

An overlooked one-movement piece which is both poetic and pictorial; many changes of tempo and special sound effects. Written originally for lutes, it has become more commonly known in an orchestral version.
> Cohn, Western Hemi-
>   sphere, 296
Parts: Union Musical Espanola
Score: Union Musical Espanola

PROKOFIEV   Quartet, string, no. 1, op. 50. 1930.
                 Comm. E. Sprague Coolidge. 24 min.
                 Adv. / Allegro. Andante-Vivace. An-
                 dante.

The soaring melodic lines of the first violin and the motor vitality of the rhythms are reminders of the composer's affinity for ballet. The three lower strings, written in a low tessitura, seem to function as a supporting unit to the soaring melodies of the first violin, much as a male dancer

might offer support to the soaring movements of the female
soloist.   There is great rhythmic independence and tension,
even in the slow sections, as the parts weave against each
other.   In three movements, only; however, the 14-bar
Andante introduction to the second serves as a contrast to
the Allegro of the first movement.   Players will encounter
frequent accidentals, rapid staccato passages, and occasional
meter changes.
    Cobbett, vol. 3, 138
Parts: Breitkopf; International; Kalmus; Music Corporation
    of America
Score: International

PROKOFIEV   Quartet, string, no. 2, op. 92, F major.
                  1942.   23 min.   Adv. / Allegro sostenuto.
                  Adagio.   Allegro.

    Subtitled "Quartet on Kabardinian Themes" this work
shows the influence of the composer's stay in the Kabardino-
Balkerian sector of the Caucasus.   The themes of the first
movement are rough and loud; the second opens with an extended plaintive song accompanied by legato triplets--when
the song changes to a gentle dance, the accompaniment also
changes to become a very effective spiccato triplet figure.
The third and final movement is another rough dance with
rapid, menacing figurations; contains a cello cadenza on a
falling scale; additional drama is achieved with effects of
pizzicato chords, col legno and sul ponticello bowing.
    Cobbett, vol. 3, 138-
      39
Parts: International; Peters 5713; Sikorski
Parts, collections: Music Corporation of America (with op.
    50)
Score: International

BEETHOVEN   Quartet, string, op. 127, E flat major.   Ded.
                Prince Galitzen.   1825.   35 min.   Adv. /
                Maestoso-Allegro.   Adagio, ma non troppo
                e molto cantabile.   Scherzando vivace.
                Finale.

    The quartets, op. 127 to op. 135 belong to Beethoven's
third or late period (1815-26).   Musicologists and critics
are reverential toward these late works--there are abundant
analyses and essays.   Opus 127 contains endless variations
of motifs which unfold in a polyphonic style akin to Bach;
with few homophonic passages and an avoidance of the sec-

tional contrasts associated with the classical sonata-allegro
form, the tender and serene themes of the first movement
seem to spring from the same germ, with little contrast between them.   A Maestoso introduction makes two dramatic
reappearances, one in G major at the beginning of the development and one in C major at the recapitulation.   The
Adagio movement is considered one of the truly sublime
theme and variations in the literature.   The Scherzo is an
extensive development of a dotted rhythm motif--its Trio is
a breathtaking Presto in six flats.   The last movement has
an extraordinary coda which arrives unexpectedly and in a
surprising tonality and shift of meter.

Cobbett, vol. 1, 99-
    101
Cooke, 30-49
Ferguson, 111-14
Fiske, 16-27
Kerman, 210-18;
    228-42

Lam, Part 2, 11-20
Marliave, 231-56
Mason, Beethoven, 163-
    82
Radcliffe, Beethoven,
    99-108
Riseling, 141-62
Scherman, 974-88

Parts: Breitkopf; Schirmer L1639
Parts, collections: Kalmus; Peters 195C; Schirmer L1879
Score: Boosey 134; Eulenberg (Peters); Universal Edition
    Ph321

BEETHOVEN   Quartet, string, op. 130, B flat major.
                1825. Ded. Nikolaus von Galitzin.   40-50
                min. Adv. / Adagio ma non troppo-Al-
                legro. Presto. Andante con moto, ma non
                troppo. (Alla danza tedesca) Allegro assai.
                (Cavatina) Adagio molto espressivo. (Finale)
                Allegro.

        A truly remarkable work which, in some listeners,
induces a more profound response than the quartet op. 131
which is considered to be the greatest.   In every movement
there are inexpressibly beautiful moments.   Daniel Gregory
Mason in his The Quartets of Beethoven says of it that it
can only gradually reveal its profound eloquence and beauty.
This is the quartet for which the "Grosse Fuge," op. 133,
was intended as a Finale.   Groups such as the Juilliard
Quartet now end the quartet with the "Grosse Fuge" which,
because of negative reactions to it, Beethoven removed, sub-
stituting a Finale (1826) which now appears as the last movement in the score but which seems to be a lesser musical
achievement.   The first movement contrasts two elements
represented by the Adagio and the Allegro; homophonic and

fugal style are integrated; the organic unfolding makes every idea seem related to every other.   There are two unique Scherzi, the first a brief "other worldly" Presto, the second an unforgettable little German dance that is gay on the surface but whose poignancy elicits sadness.   The spacious themes of the third movement are enhanced by staccato contrapuntal movement; Mason describes this spaciousness as "... slow, not through the burden of sadness or the delving of thought, but to accommodate the amplitude of its happy leisure. "   By contrast, the Cavatina is an unrivalled expression of anguish, especially in the middle section of the song marked "Beklemmt," which means "oppressed. "

Cobbett, vol. 1, 102-4
Cooke, 30-49
Ferguson, 114-18
Fiske, 28-46
Kerman, 303-25; 367-
    74
Lam, Part 2, 34-52

Marliave, 197-231; 256-
    93
Mason, Beethoven, 208-
    28
Radcliffe, Beethoven,
    123-37
Riseling, 141-62
Scherman, 971-74; 989-
    93.

Parts: Breitkopf
Parts, collections: Kalmus; Peters 195C; Schirmer L1879
Score: Breitkopf; Eulenberg; Heugel; Ricordi; Universal Edition

BEETHOVEN   Quartet, string, op. 131, C sharp minor.
                 1826.   Ded. Baron Joseph von Stutterheim.
                 35 min.   Adv. / Adagio, ma non troppo
                 e molto espressivo-Allegro molto vivace-
                 Allegro moderato-Andante, ma non troppo e
                 molto cantabile-Presto-Adagio quasi un poco
                 andante-Allegro.

Beethoven chose to open the C sharp minor quartet with a fugue and to close it in a sonata-allegro form.   The movements are not labeled as such but are numbered parts which segue one into the next.   The somber fugal theme of the first part is treated freely and in several keys before activity ceases and all parts are poised on C sharp.   As they slip upward to D the second section begins, establishing a new mood in the key of D major.   It is based on the travels of a rising octave motif through many tonal regions.   The third section, which combines punctuated, staccato groupings with a violin cadenza is brief and transitional; the fourth section is a set of variations on a simple theme (presented by both violins) which remains, almost to the end, in its opening

tonality of A major.   The fifth section, Presto, is light and
simple, its opening theme a staccato one and its secondary
theme legato.   There are playful pauses and ritards, changes
of dynamics, and an effective sul ponticello ending.   Section
six, transitional like the third section, is a brief lament.
The driving motto theme of the C sharp minor Finale gives
it an intense and energized feel, mitigated somewhat by the
second subject's breadth and its presentation in the contrasting major mode.

Cobbett, vol. 1, 105   Marliave, 197-231; 295-
Cooke, 30-49   328
Ferguson, 118-22   Mason, Beethoven, 239-
Fiske, 46-58   67
Kerman, 325-49   Radcliffe, Beethoven,
Lam, Part 2, 52-65   148-64
                              Riseling, 141-62
                              Scherman, 971-74; 994-
                                 1001

Parts: Breitkopf
Parts, collections: Kalmus; Peters 195C; Schirmer L1879
Score: Breitkopf; Eulenberg; Heugel; Ricordi; Universal Edi-
   tion

BEETHOVEN   Quartet, string, op. 132, A minor.   1825.
               Ded. Nikolaus von Galitzin.   38 to 47 min.
               Adv.   /   Assai sostenuto-Allegro.   (Heiliger
               Dankgesang eines Genesenen an die Gottheit,
               in der lydischen Tonart) Molto adagio-(Neue
               Kraft fühlend) Andante.   Alla marcia, assai
               vivace.   Allegro appassionato.

        The most sublime moments of op. 132, which Beetho-
ven wrote after op. 127, are contained in its slow movement
which Beethoven inscribed as "A Holy Song of Thanksgiving
to the Godhead from a Convalescent, in the Lydian mode."
The choice of this mode adds to the prayerfulness of the opening statement which moves in only half or quarter notes.
The Andante section which follows contains much more activity and conveys a sense of vitality, of well-being.   The
Adagio and Andante appear again in tandem, each greatly en-
riched either melodically or contrapuntally.   The movement
ends with a third appearance of the Adagio, this time with
still more elaboration and marked "With inmost feeling."
This centerpiece movement is preceded by a delicate Scherzo
and followed by a delicate March; the March is separated
from the Finale by a recitative section and violin quasi-cadenza.   The joyful affirmation of the final movement, with

its lilting melody, contrasts greatly with the restlessness
and anxiety of the first movement. Each of the movements
has a motif which comes to the fore and dominates; the quartet as a whole is highly unified and displays Beethoven's
masterful handling of germinal growth of a musical idea.

Cobbett, vol. 1, 101-2   Marliave, 197-231; 328-
Cooke, 30-49   35
Ferguson, 122-26   Mason, Beethoven,
Fiske, 59-70   183-207
Kerman, 242-68   Radcliffe, Beethoven,
Lam, Part 2, 20-34   109-22
                                Riseling, 141-62
                                Scherman, 971-74;
                                    1001-1004

Parts: Breitkopf
Parts, collections: Kalmus; Peters 195C; Schirmer L1879
Score: Breitkopf; Eulenberg; Heugel; Ricordi; Universal Edi-
     tion

BEETHOVEN   Quartet, string, op. 133, "Grosse Fuge."
                1825. Ded. Kardinal Erzherzog. 18 min.
                Adv. / (Overtura) Allegro-Allegro-Fuga.

The "Great Fugue," intended as a finale to op. 130,
cannot fail to impress the listener with its fierceness and
fury. When there was a strong negative reaction to its
length, ruggedness, tonal clashings, and unmanageability in
terms of string technique, it was withdrawn by Beethoven,
who substituted another. There are five sections: the Over-
tura which presents the germinal theme; the first fugue, a
double fugue using the germinal theme as its counter subject;
the second fugue which is in a more tranquil mood and which
presents a second subject in conjunction with the theme (in
G flat major); the third fugue which is a Scherzo treatment
of the theme combined with a third subject; and the Coda
which brings back the first subject. Many professional quartets are now presenting op. 133 in its original position as a
final movement to op. 130.

Cobbett, vol. 1, 104-5   Mason, Beethoven, 229-
Cooke, 30-49   38
Ferguson, 126-28   Radcliffe, Beethoven,
Fiske, 39-46   138-47
Kerman, 269-95   Riseling, 141-62
Lam, Part 2, 44-52   Scherman, 971-74;
Marliave, 197-231;   1013-16
    293-95

Parts: Breitkopf
Parts, collections: Kalmus; Peters 195C; Schirmer L1879

Score: Breitkopf; Eulenberg; Heugel; Ricordi; Universal Edition

BEETHOVEN   Quartet, string, op. 135, F major. 1826.
                  Ded. Johann Wolfmayer. 22 min. Adv. /
                  Allegretto. Vivace. Lento assai, cantate
                  e tranquillo. (Der schwer gefasste Entsch-
                  luss) Grave, ma non troppo tratto-Allegro.

        Beethoven returns to the more traditional classical
form for his last quartet. It is shorter and, in its way,
simpler than the other late quartets. The first movement
is based on several thematic fragments, but the first one
presented is the one that dominates. The Scherzo is homophonic in texture, with long passages of repeated tones or
unison ostinati--there are unexpected harmonic shifts, and
in the Trio the first violin hops about frantically on wide
intervals. A brief and tender Lento follows. The last movement, over which Beethoven wrote "The difficult question,"
contains two motifs, the first marked Grave over which
Beethoven wrote "Muss es sein?" ("Must it be?") and the second, marked Allegro, over which he wrote "Es muss sein!"
("It must be!"). Throughout the movement he exploits the
question-answer situation.

        Cobbett, vol. 1, 105-6   Mason, Beethoven,
        Cooke, 30-49   268-83
        Ferguson, 128-31   Radcliffe, Beethoven,
        Fiske, 70-77   165-74
        Kerman, 354-67   Riseling, 141-62
        Lam, Part 2, 65-72   Scherman, 971-74;
        Marliave, 197-231;   1004-13
          355-79

Parts: Breitkopf; Schirmer L1643
Parts, collections: Kalmus; Peters 195C; Schirmer L1879
Score: Breitkopf; Eulenberg; Heugel; Ricordi; Universal Edi-
        tion

SCHOENBERG   Quartet, string, no. 4, op. 37. 1936. 33
                  min. Adv. + / Allegro molto. Energico.
                  Comodo. Largo. Allegro.

        This is intense and rigorously constructed, but it has
a very refined texture which calls for playing with delicacy
and finesse. It is lyrical rather than pointillistic. All the
instruments share in the musical tasks--no one predominates.
The Largo is particularly arresting, sounding like a lamenta-
tion with all the strings playing in unison. The score and

parts are annotated carefully, so that players are informed
of which themes are important and which are secondary; the
parts are carefully marked also for dynamic levels and kinds
of accents.

Cobbett, vol. 3, 1-3   Whittall, 50-55
Cohn, Europe, 267
Parts: Schirmer
Score: Schirmer

BERG   Lyrische (Lyric) Suite, string quartet.
                1925-26. Ded. Alexander Zemlinsky. 40
                min. Adv. + / Allegretto giovale. An-
                dante amoroso. Allegro misterioso-Trio
                estatico. Adagio appassionato. Presto
                delirando-Tenebroso. Largo desolato.

One of the greatest and most dramatic chamber works
of the century, it makes heavy demands on the musicians.
All the resources of string technique are called upon.   In
the outer movements Berg uses strict 12-tone serial technique,
but a freer kind of atonality in the middle movements.   An
example of the drama in the piece is the ghostly scurrying
of the Allegro misterioso followed by the loud and intense
Trio estatico.   Another example of drama is that the slow
movements become slower as the suite progresses, and the
fast movements become faster, having a distinct psychological
effect upon the listener.

Carner, 109-23   Ferguson, 296-301
Cobbett, vol. 1, 120-   Redlich, Berg, 137-54
    21   Robertson, 400-405
Cohn, Europe, 41-42
Parts: Universal Edition 8781
Score: Universal Edition Ph173

WEBERN   Satze (Pieces), string quartet, op. 5. 1909.
                10 min. Adv. + / Heftig bewegt. Sehr
                langsam. Sehr bewegt. Sehr langsam.
                In zarter Bewegung.

These are so carefully wrought within Webern's realm
of musical structure that it is not easy to perceive how he
proceeds; however, the intensity and emotional content are
readily apparent.   It is a desolate sounding work which seems
to be a distillation of music materials, just as a visual work
of art can be abstract.   It utilizes various technical and musical resources of the players.   There is an excellent article
on serial music in the second edition of the Harvard Dictio-

nary of Music for those who would like to learn more about
the 20th-century Viennese school.

    Cobbett, vol. 2, 571-   Kolneder, 53-58
      73
    Ferguson, 301-4
Parts: Universal Edition 5889
Score: Universal Edition Ph358

BLOCH   Quartet, string, no. 2. 1945. Ded. Alex
              Cohen. 33 min. Adv. / Moderato.
              Presto. Andante. Allegro molto.

    An intense, almost savage work, tightly organized,
organically unified, and rhythmically forthright. Bloch takes
one motif and treats it in a variety of ways, including its
use as a basis for the Passacaglia and the Fugue of the last
movement. There is a little melismatic figure which appears
in the violin solo at the beginning of the quartet and which
makes reappearances throughout. The Hebraic cast associated with Bloch's compositions is in evidence in the choice
of exotic scales and their harmonizations and in its brooding
quality. Because it is long and intense it makes demands
on the players' concentration ability and endurance.

    Cobbett, vol. 3, 182-   Ferguson, 325
      84
    Cohn, Western Hemi-
      sphere, 36-37
Parts: Boosey
Score: Boosey

MILHAUD   Quartets, string, no. 14; no. 15. 1949.
              Ded. Paul Collaer. 17 min. Adv. /
              Animé. Modéré. Vif.

    When Milhaud received a gift book containing 84 pages
of blank music paper with two sets of four staves on each
page he conceived the idea of filling up the book with two
quartets which could be played separately or combined--a
situation analogous to an 18th-century composer setting himself the task of writing a multi-voiced fugue and having to
deal with the qualifications assigned to the musical material.
Each of the movements of both quartets has intricate, active
parts, so the octet has a rather thick texture and Milhaud's
use of polytonality adds to the complexity of sound. The
Animé movements complement each other--that of no. 14 is
lyrical and that of no. 15 is brisk. The Modérés blend
most effectively--each has a thin texture and a more subdued, somber cast. The Vif movements create more of a

jumble--no. 14 is a piquant polytonal treatment of French
folk tunes and no. 15 is full of Brazilian rhythms and syncopations.
    Cobbett, vol. 3, 31-32   Mason, Milhaud, 326-41
Parts: Heugel
Score: Heugel

MALIPIERO   Quartet, string, "Rispetti e Strambotti."
               1920. Ded. Madame Frederic S. Coolidge.
               20 min. Adv.

An attractive, contemporary sounding work in a style
somewhere between Ravel and early Bartók. It would make
a good introduction for those not conversant with these composers and it is without technical problems aside from many
accidentals and an occasional portamento. The viola part
is prominent occasionally with some mellifluous passages in
the treble clef. The form is unusual--a series of 20 stanzas
with a connecting theme of chords on open strings. Texture,
length, style, and tempos change from one stanza to another.
In the quartet, which won the Coolidge prize in 1920, the
composer attempts to capture the spirit of early bucolic Italian verse. The quintal sonorities contribute to the rusticism.
    Cobbett, vol. 2, 110-   Cohn, Europe, 184
      11; vol. 3, 51; 53-
      54
Parts: Chester; Ricordi
Score: Chester; Ricordi

IVES   Quartet, string, no. 1, "A Revival Service."
               1896. 20 min. Int. to Adv. / (Fugue)
               Andante con moto. (Prelude) Allegro. (Of-
               fertory) Adagio cantabile. (Postlude) Allegro
               marziale.

Ives, while a church organist, used the first three
movements as an organ service. The first movement was
finally united with them and the quartet was published in 1961.
Ives was extraordinary in his time--a truly original composer
who invoked the hymns and tunes that he heard while growing
up in New England. He also tried to recreate the mood of
childhood experiences. His second string quartet (1907-13)
has movements labeled "Discussions," "Arguments," and
"The Call of the Mountains." The opening movement of the
first quartet is a fugue on a hymn tune, in C major and in
a 4/2 meter; the other movements are tripartite with a shift
of meter or tonality in the contrasting sections. Simple key
signatures are employed. An example of Ives' uniqueness

is the juxtaposition of 3/4 and 4/4 meters near the close of
the final movement.   Purchase of both quartets is recommended.

Bader, 292-95   Cohn, Western Hemi-
Cobbett, vol. 3, 153   sphere, 141-42 (quar-
                                  tet no. 2)
Parts: Peer
Score: Peer

BARTÓK   Quartet, string, no. 3. 1927. Ded. Mu-
                      sical Fund Society of Philadelphia. 15 min.
                      Adv. + / (Prima parte) Moderato. (Sec-
                      onda parte) Allegro. (Recapitulazione della
                      prima parte) Moderato. (Coda) Allegro
                      molto.

    The third quartet is actually a single movement with
four sections; it is filled with exotic sounds ranging from
ethereal to barbaric.   There are passages of concerted glissandi, pizzicato double stops, sul ponticello, col legno, and
punta d'arco; there is much dissonance and syncopation.
The quartet is constructed in arch form with a barbaric Allegro as the keystone.   Bartók presents just a few motifs
throughout which are constantly subject to a free canonic or
imitative treatment.

Cohn, Europe, 28; 29-   Monelle, 70-81
    30   Stevens, 183-86
Ferguson, 279-82
Króo, 137-41
Parts: Boosey; Universal Edition
Score: Universal Edition Ph169

BARTÓK   Quartet, string, no. 4. 1928. Ded. Pro
                      Arte Quartet. 22 min.   Adv. + / Allegro.
                      Prestissimo con sordino. Non troppo lento.
                      Allegretto pizzicato. Allegro molto.

    The fourth quartet makes heavy demands on the players
--there are many glissandi and unusual pizzicato effects.   It
is the most exotic "other world"-sounding quartet, especially
the third movement, which presents a barren landscape referred to in Bartók's compositions as "night music."   It begins with eerie sustained chords which serve as a background
to a rhapsodic cello solo.   In keeping with the arch form,
the first and fifth movements and the second and fourth are
linked motivically.   Bartók's motifs throughout are drawn
out, inverted, and elaborated in a marvel of canonic weaving.
Even long ostinato passages are treated canonically.   Melodic

intervals are often combined harmonically. There is much
syncopation, especially in the second and fourth scherzi
movements.

Cohn, Europe, 28; 30   Monelle, 70-81
Ferguson, 282-85   Stevens, 186-91
Króo, 150-55
Parts: Boosey
Score: Universal Edition Ph166

BARTÓK   Quartet, string, no. 5. 1934. Ded. Mrs.
                Sprague-Coolidge. 28 min. Adv. + / Al-
                legro. Adagio molto. Scherzo. Andante.
                (Finale) Allegro vivace.

The fifth quartet is structured like the fourth, an
arch form with five movements; however, the central movement, rather than a Lento, is a Scherzo in a Bulgarian rhythm. Perhaps not as closely knit as the fourth, its movements are linked in the same way, the first and last motivically, and the second and fourth structurally. Most of the
typical characteristics of Bartók are evident--expansions and
inversions of motivic fragments, frequent appearance of the
tritone, complex counterpoint, cross rhythms and syncopation,
the folk flavor of rhythms, scales, and the drone-like passages, ostinati passages, unusual timbre effects, and the
general freedom of tonality.

Cohn, Europe, 28; 31   Monelle, 70-81
Ferguson, 273-92   Stevens, 191-97
Króo, 172-80
Parts: Boosey; Universal Edition
Score: Universal Edition Ph167

BARTÓK   Quartet, string, no. 6. 1939. Ded. Kolisch
                Quartet. 26 min. Adv. + / Mesto-Più
                mosso, pesante-Vivace. Mesto-Marcia.
                Mesto-(Burletta) Moderato. Mesto.

In his last quartet Bartók, instead of employing the
arch form, uses a motto theme as a unifying factor. The
theme, always marked Mesto, which means "sad," appears
at the beginning of every movement and is the thematic foundation for the entire final movement. The quartet opens with
13 bars of the motto theme for viola alone; before the second
movement it appears as a cello solo against muted tremolo
octaves, and before the third in a three-part setting. Its
appearance in the fourth movement is marked by a canon at
the tritone (an augmented fourth interval). In the inner
movements there are more coloristic and folk devices than

in the outer movements.   The Marcia, reminiscent of the
"Verbunkos" of <u>Contrasts</u> for piano, clarinet, and violin, is
based on a dotted rhythm pattern in close imitation.   After
a Trio section which contains many tremolo thirds, pizzicato
chords, and a transitional ostinati passage, there is an eerie
recapitulation of the Marcia theme in harmonic double stops,
in fourths combined with octave, fifth, and sixth interval
double stops.   For the sometimes grotesque Burletta, in
addition to his usual coloristic effects, the composer has the
two violins playing glissando thirds with the second violin
tuned down a quarter tone.

Cohn, <u>Europe</u>, 28; 31-   Monelle, 70-81
    32   Stevens, 197-203
Ferguson, 273-92
Króo, 215-21
Parts: Boosey
Score: Boosey

HINDEMITH   Quartet, string, no. 5, E flat major.   1943.
                    Ded. Budapest String Quartet.   25 min.
                    Adv. / Very quiet and expressive.   Lively
                    and very energetic.   Quiet, Variations.
                    Lively, gay.

    Highly regarded for its thematic ingenuity--in the
last movement all the main themes of the quartet are ab-
sorbed into the thematic texture; analysis reveals Hindemith's
procedures as closely knit and economical.   The first movement is an introductory fugue in which the subject eventually
appears as a theme in homophonic texture.   The second movement opens with a unison theme followed by monothematic
interplay and canonic treatment.   Material from the first
movement is juxtaposed with the unison theme.   The third
movement is a set of variations ending in a lively march.
The perfect intervals which are Hindemith trademarks dominate the textures, melodically and harmonically, of the last
two movements.

Cobbett, vol. 3, 13-14   Mason, <u>Hindemith</u>, 150-
Ferguson, 294-95   55
Parts: Schott 2277
Score: Schott 3537

SEEGER   Quartet, string.   1931.   12 min.   Adv. /
                    Rubato assai.   Leggiero, tempo giusto.
                    Andante.   Allegro possible.

    In 1930 Ruth Crawford Seeger became the first woman
to be awarded a Guggenheim Fellowship.   This quartet was

written in Berlin the next year and was published ten years later by New Music. There are many unusual aspects--the third movement has been called a "counterpoint of dynamic pulsations" in which there are gradual crescendi and decrescendi on long tones. The textures are thin with many passages written for only two or three voices. The first movement has complex divisions of the beat; the last contains an extended violin solo against a single line played by the other instruments in double octaves.
 Cobbett, vol. 3, 180-81
Parts: New Music Edition
Score: New Music Edition

BARBER   Quartet, string, op. 11. 1936. Ded.
        Louise and Sydney Homer. 18 min. Adv.
        / Molto allegro e appassionato. Molto
        adagio.

 An anachronistic work in two movements--at the close of the second there is a brief recapitulation of the first which gives the impression of a third movement. The first opens with a vigorous unison theme whose characteristic rhythm dominates. A chorale section follows and then the solo violin introduces a tranquil theme in a homophonic setting. The material is developed and repeated. The Adagio has become famous on its own and is often heard in the arrangement which the composer made for string orchestra.
  Cobbett, vol. 3, 168   Cohn, Western Hemi-
              sphere, 21
Parts: Schirmer
Score: Schirmer

REGER   Quartet, string, no. 4, op. 109, E flat
        major. Pub. 1909. Ded. Adolf Wach. 34
        min. Adv. / Allegro molto. Quasi pres-
        to. Larghetto. Allegro con grazia e con
        spirito.

 Those who feel that Reger's compositions wander aimlessly and are also uninspired might find this opus a redeeming one, with its nice textural changes in the first movement, its great intensity in the slow movement, and its masterful counterpoint in the fugue of the last. Parts are typical of Reger--active, highly chromatic, and with unusual melodic configurations that can confound even the best of sight readers.
  Cobbett, vol. 2, 281-82
Parts: Bote & Bock
Score: Eulenberg (Peters E293)

SHOSTAKOVICH   Quartet, string, no. 7, op. 108, F sharp
                    minor. 1960. Ded. Nina Vasilyevna
                    Shostakovich. 13 min. Adv. / Alle-
                    gretto. Lento. Allegro.

Considered a turning point in Shostakovich's style;
texture is sparse, as in his first quartet, often for only one
or two voices at a time; in many passages the inner strings
play accompanimental, harmonized repeated staccato sixteenth
notes while outer voices double a melodic line; use of thematic material is economical--a great deal of mileage is
gained through repetition, rather than organic development of
a motif. The first movement consists of two alternating
motifs presented in a crisp, concise style. The middle
movement is muted and is characterized by a long legato
sixteenth-note accompanimental figure. The last movement
is a fugue based on a staccato motif. Its frenzied effect
gives way to a delicate waltz and the work comes to a gentle
close.
        Cobbett, vol. 3, 148-49
Parts: MZK; Musica Rara; Sikorski R6204
Score: Eulenberg (Peters E391); MZK; Musica Rara; Sikorski R6219

SHOSTAKOVICH   Quartet, string, no. 13, op. 138, B flat
                    minor. Ded. Vadim Borisovsky. 20 min.
                    Adv. / Adagio-Doppio movimento-Tempo
                    primo.

The mood is desolate; a rather stark one-movement
work with a midsection where the tempo is doubled; opening
tonality of six flats is unusual. The important intervals are
heard at the start in the viola. The first section is a homophonic chorale but with an intense climax out of character;
the second section, announced by a staccato motif in the violin, contains sudden crescendi and harsh chords. A pervasive
rhythmic figure appears along with occasional startling knock-
ing sounds (made by striking the belly of the instrument with
the bow stick). The staccato motif reappears, followed by
the viola which announces the recapitulation. The work comes
to a subdued ending with the viola solo and the knocks on
wood. The work was dedicated to the violist of the Beethoven
Quartet.
Parts: MZK
Score: MZK

SIBELIUS   Quartet, string, op. 56, D minor, "Voces intimae. " 1909. 27 min. Adv. / Andante-Allegro molto moderato. Vivace. Adagio di molto. Allegretto, ma pesante. Allegro.

There is less evidence than one would expect of the symphonist in Sibelius' only string quartet. It does not fit the standard mold either in outward form or internal design. It is like a suite, with each of five movements an organic unfolding of one idea rather than a series of contrasting themes. Thus, the same mood is sustained through each movement. The Scherzo is noteworthy for chains of triplets from start to finish and the Vivace for its persistent tremolo. The low tessitura gives a certain low-key emotional cast.
　　Cobbett, vol. 2, 416-19
Parts: International; Kalmus; Robert Lienau (Peters R20)
Score: Eulenberg (Peters E294)

BRIDGE　　　　Quartet, string, no. 3. 1926. Ded. Elizabeth Sprague Coolidge. 28 min. Adv. / Andante moderato-Allegro moderato. Andante con moto. Allegro energico.

Bridge, a sensitive composer, whose works are finely crafted, has been terribly neglected. His third and fourth (1937) string quartets show a dramatic shift from an earlier, more traditional, romantic style to one, although of a lyrical nature, showing a strong Alban Berg influence. There is great clarity in the contrapuntal writing and an overall expressiveness. Information is lacking about availability of parts for this quartet. The score is available from Augener, as is the score and parts for the first quartet.
Parts: information unavailable
Score: Augener

VAUGHAN WILLIAMS Quartet, string, no. 2, A minor, "For Jean on Her Birthday." 1944. Ded. Jean Stewart of the Menges Quartet. 25 min. Adv. / (Prelude) Allegro appassionato. (Romance) Largo. (Scherzo) Allegro. (Epilogue) Andante sostenuto.

Violists will want a "crack" at this quartet, dedicated to one. Every movement begins with a viola solo and the viola part remains important throughout. The title of the first movement belies its extensive development. In the

Scherzo three strings play a unison line against the viola
and in the same movement there are parts for muted strings,
sul ponticello, and much tremolo. The last movement is
subtitled "Greetings from Joan to Jean" because the theme
is from a projected score of the composer for a film on
Joan of Arc.
>   Cobbett, vol. 3, 82-84
Parts: Oxford University Press
Score: Oxford University Press

VALEN   Quartet, string, no. 2, op. 13. 1931. 15
                 min. Adv. / Andante con moto. Tempo
                 di menuetto, grazioso. (Finale) Allegro
                 assai.

     Valen, a Norwegian, developed a dodecaphonic style
of his own in the 1920's, based on an elaboration of motifs
and themes, which did not appeal to the folk-oriented Norwegian musical public. Recognition did not come until the
1940's, and then from outside Norway. Today he has a
small but universal group of champions, one of whom, Bjarne
Kortsen, has included a detailed description of this quartet
in his Modern Norwegian Chamber Music. A recording is
available on the Argo label (RG-81).
>   Cobbett, vol. 3, 80-81   Kortsen, Valen, 125;
>   Kortsen, Modern Nor-   136-43
>   wegian, 138-65
Parts: Norsk Musikförlag
Score: Norsk Musikförlag

CARTER   Quartet, string, no. 1. 1951. 25 min.
                 Adv. + / (Fantasia) Maestoso-Allegro scor-
                 revole. Allegro scorrevole-Adagio.

     Elliott Carter is a wonderfully gifted American com-
poser whose compositions are tremendously difficult to prepare. Carter himself refers to this quartet as a "continuous
unfolding and changing of expressive characters" and made
up of "many-layered contrasts of character. " The first
movement opens with a cello cadenza which serves as an
introduction and which reappears at the end of the work as
a final variation. Cohn describes the work as innovative in
the use of permutative rhythm designed to function with thematic content as a second dimension of continuity.
>   Cohn, Western Hemi-
>   sphere, 40-42
Parts: Associated Music Publishers
Score: Associated Music Publishers

(4) PIANO QUARTETS

*MOZART   Quartet, piano, no. 1, K. 478, G minor.
                 1785. 25 min. Adv. / Allegro. An-
                 dante. (Rondo) Allegro.

     Mozart's two masterpieces for piano quartet, K. 478,
and K. 493 in E flat major, were not readily accepted by
his public because they were more advanced, conceptually
and technically. In moving away from concerto style, he
freed the strings from an accompanimental role and consequently made the parts more difficult. Structurally, the
three movement quartets are similar, but as one might de-
duce from the key signatures, the G minor is weighty while
the E flat is sunny and more transparent in texture. Counter
melodies and melodic embroideries are exquisite. In the
second quartet the strings play more distinctive roles in
many imitative passages while in the first they function as a
unit in concertante fashion. Purchase of both in one volume
is recommended.
     Cobbett, vol. 2, 167-   Ferguson, 55-56
        68   King, 33-35
     Einstein, Mozart, 263-
        65
Parts: Augener; Breitkopf
Parts, collections: Durand (with K. 493); Peters 272 (with
     K. 493)
Score: Eulenberg (Peters E158); Lea 90 (with K. 452, K.
     493)

*BRAHMS   Quartet, piano, no. 1, op. 25, G minor.
                 Pub. 1863. Ded. Reinhard von Dalwigk.
                 38 min. Adv. / Allegro. (Intermezzo)
                 Allegro ma non troppo. Andante con moto.
                 (Rondo alla Zingarese) Presto.

     An exciting, impassioned work, exhibiting a wealth of
invention; its final movement, the Gypsy Rondo is one of the
most exciting in the literature--its main theme is combined
with contrasting episodes, which are either scurrying, fiery,
or sentimental; just before the close, there is a cadenza for
piano alternating with one for strings. The first movement
is tightly knit, its three themes developed extensively. The
pathos of the second movement is heightened in the passages
for strings alone, strings in unison, and in the hushed piano
entrances--the movement has a strange lilt, its two rather

tragic themes cast in a triple meter framework.   The third,
in ternary form, contains a notable march theme.

Cobbett, vol. 1, 167;   Ferguson, 193-95
  168-69   Keys, 14-16
Colles, 17-18   Mason, Brahms, 22-32
Drinker, 73-76   Tovey, Chamber Music,
Evans, vol. 1, 96-   185-93
  119

Parts: Breitkopf; Peters 3939A
Parts, collections: Henle 276 (with op. 26, op. 60)
Score: Eulenberg (Peters E240); Peters (Brahms Chamber
  Music, vol. 2)

BRAHMS   Quartet, piano, op. 26, A major.   Pub.
1863.   Ded.   Frau Dr. Elisabeth Rösing.
45 min.   Adv.   / Allegro non troppo.
Poco Adagio.   (Scherzo) Poco Allegro.
(Finale) Allegro.

This quartet might be considered the feminine counterpart to the op. 25 quartet--it is in a much lighter vein and
with fewer dramatic contrasts.   Its length has been criticized
by some who feel that the thematic material is too ordinary
for the extensive development it receives.   The Adagio is
extraordinary.   The strings are muted at the outset and play
a rocking eighth-note accompaniment to the piano theme.
This rocking pattern immediately becomes important as a
thematic motif.   In between statements of the cantabile theme
are unusual episodes made out of curving, harp-like piano
arpeggios on diminished or minor chords.   Brahms treats
the strings as one unit in dialogue with the piano.

Cobbett, vol. 1, 167;   Ferguson, 195-97
  169-70   Keys, 17-20
Colles, 19-21   Mason, Brahms, 33-42
Drinker, 87-90   Tovey, Chamber Music,
Evans, vol. 1, 121-   194-202
  36

Parts: Breitkopf; Peters 3939B
Parts, collections: Henle 276 (with op. 25, op. 60)
Score: Eulenberg (Peters E241); Peters (Brahms Chamber
  Music, vol. 2)

BRAHMS   Quartet, piano, op. 60, C minor.   Pub.
1875.   30 min.   Adv.   / Allegro non troppo.   (Scherzo) Allegro.   Andante.   (Finale)
Allegro comodo.

Brahms was supposed to have begun work on this before op. 25 and op. 26; its original key was C sharp minor and the key of the Andante (E major) is a leftover from that original key. The work has a tragic cast; the first movement has a long, introductory statement which turns out to be a variation of the upcoming first theme. The Scherzo is vigorous and rhythmically complex; the third movement is based on an eloquent song which begins as a cello solo and gathers intensity as the other instruments join in; the last movement, except for periodic chorale sections, is vigorous, with a perpetual-motion eighth-note figure predominating.

Cobbett, vol. 1, 174-   Ferguson, 193; 197-98
   75   Keys, 20-22
Colles, 36-40   Mason, Brahms, 108-11
Drinker, 116-19   Tovey, Chamber Music,
Evans, vol. 1, 255-   203-14
   74

Parts: Breitkopf; International; Peters 3939C
Parts, collections: Henle 276
Score: Eulenberg (Peters E242); Peters (Brahms Chamber Music, vol. 2)

SCHUMANN   Quartet, piano, op. 47, E flat major. 1842.
                Ded. Count Mathieu Wielhorsky. 25 min.
                Adv. / Sostenuto assai-Allegro ma non
                troppo. (Scherzo) Molto vivace. Andante
                cantabile. (Finale) Vivace.

A work of great vitality which may translate into exhaustion for the players; there are rapid staccato passages throughout, except for the Andante, a beautiful movement in which a cantabile solo is taken up by each of the strings in turn while the others weave countermelodies or melodic decorations; the piano part is accompanimental. At the close of the movement the cello C string is tuned down to B flat for the final chord. The Finale is exuberant with alternating fugal and lyrical sections. The overall effect tends to thickness.

Cobbett, vol. 2, 371;   Ferguson, 168-70
   382-86

Parts: Breitkopf; International; Peters 2380
Score: Eulenberg (Peters E77)

FAURÉ   Quartet, piano, op. 15, C minor. 1879.
                30 min. Int.-Adv. / Allegro molto moderato. (Scherzo) Allegro vivo. Adagio.
                Allegro molto.

Fauré's compositions have been neglected, perhaps

because he was not an innovator during a time of musical innovation. This is a beautiful work, not too difficult, and one that will enhance the comparatively limited repertoire for piano quartet. Fauré wrote another piano quartet in G minor (op. 45); it is considered superior to op. 15, but somehow, somewhat less appealing. The work (op. 15) could be described as poignant in mood and kaleidoscopic in its harmonies.

    Cobbett, vol. 1, 387-90   Robertson, 374-76
    Ferguson, 252-54
Parts, collections: Hamelle (with op. 45); International (with op. 45)
Score: Hamelle

DVOŘÁK   Quartet, piano, op. 87 (B. 162), E flat major. 1889. 34 min. Adv. / Allegro con fuoco. Lento. (Scherzo) Allegro moderato, grazioso. (Finale) Allegro ma non troppo.

    Dvořák's quartet has many shifting harmonies, especially in the Finale; noteworthy aspects are the gypsy flavor of the third movement in the harmonic minor mode, the opening and close of the first movement (the strings in unison and string tremolo), and the structure of the second movement. It has two parts with five themes repeated in each part. There is also a beautiful cello solo in this movement.

    Cobbett, vol. 1, 368   Sourek, 130-37
    Ferguson, 231-32
Parts: Artia; International; Simrock
Score: Artia; Eulenberg (Peters E330)

MENDELSSOHN   Quartets, piano, op. 1, C minor; op. 2, F minor; op. 3, B minor. 1822-24. 20 min. each. Int.-Adv.

    Intermediate level for strings, more advanced for piano--string parts are often sustained melodies or harmonies against rapid scales or arpeggiations for piano. The Scherzo of op. 1 makes demands on the pianist's velocity; its Trio section is unique in that the pianist uses the left hand alone to form one of the voices in a slow chorale. The three quartets show Mendelssohn's grasp of classical form and are worthy of an occasional reading, especially op. 3, which is considered most consistent in quality.

    Cobbett, vol. 2, 130-31   Radcliffe, Mendelssohn,
    Horton, 14-17   89-102
Parts: Peters 1741

(4) WIND QUARTETS

CARTER   Eight Etudes and a Fantasy, fl, ob, cl, bsn.
                   1950. Ded. Richard Franko Goldman. 23
                   min. Adv. / Maestoso. Quietly. Adagio
                   possible. Vivace. Andante. Allegretto.
                   Intensely. Presto. Fantasy.

     Serious and challenging; most of the etudes consist of
rapidly moving parts which dovetail quite a bit; some of the
intervallic relationships create awkward fingering patterns;
there are scampering and chattering effects, passages of
tremolo and flutter tonguing, a few harmonic fingerings.
The third and the seventh etudes, the slow ones, provide unusual contrasts--the third is a series of dovetailed notes in
a continuously sounding chord and the seventh is one continuously sounding pitch (F) with subtle variation of timbre
and volume as the instruments enter and leave. The Fantasy
is an extensively developed contrapuntal exercise--clarinet
and bassoon begin a fugue, followed by flute; quite a bit of
momentum is built up by the three instruments before the
oboe enters.
     Cohn, Western Hemi-
        sphere, 40; 41-42
Parts: Associated Music Publishers
Score: Associated Music Publishers

FRANÇAIX   Quartet, fl, ob, cl, bsn. 1955. Ded.
                   Quintette à vent de Paris. 12 min. Adv.
                   / Allegro. Andante. Allegro molto.
                   Allegro vivo.

     A polished work with a great deal of rhythmic inter-
play and rapid articulations. The mood is sunny, the style
urbane. Numerous challenges include quick tempi, dovetailing rapid figurations, a bassoon part with rapid leaping
intervals and a flute part with passages in the extreme registers.
Parts: Schott
Score: Schott 4424

BRIDGE   Divertimento, fl, ob, cl, bsn. Pub. 1940.
                   Ded. Mrs. Elisabeth S. Coolidge. 18 min.
                   Adv. / (Prelude) Allegro animato ma non
                   troppo. (Nocturne) Poco lento-Allegretto
                   capriccioso. (Scherzetto) Allegro gajo.
                   (Bagatelle) Allegro con moto.

Well structured; makes imaginative use of wind timbres
and capabilities; inner movements are duets--the Nocturne
for flute and oboe, the Scherzetto for clarinet and bassoon.
Parts are challenging for sight reading, but pose no problems
otherwise. Bridge was an English composer who wrote in
the idiom of Schoenberg, but whose early works are in a
traditional vein; his string quartets are excellent works which
have been neglected, unfortunately.
Parts: Boosey; Musica Rara
Score: Boosey

BERGER   Quartet, fl, ob, cl, bsn, C major. Ded.
                    Aaron Copland. 10 min. Adv. / Allegro
                    moderato. Andante. Allegro vivace e leg-
                    germente.

Idiomatic writing in a contrapuntal style with a nice
balance of legato and staccato--a legato line in one part is
often juxtaposed with a staccato line in another. The theme
of the first movement is presented first in a 2/4 meter and
then in 6/8; there is a calm section in six flats. A recom-
mendation by Virgil Thompson appears on the score "... tunes
are magnificently simple, its contrapuntal writing witty and
apt, its architectural makeup ample and easy...."
Parts: Peters 6034
Score: Peters 6035

STAMITZ   Quartet, ob, cl, hn, bsn, op. 8, no. 2, E
                    flat major. Pub. 1785? 10 min. Int.-
                    Adv. / Allegro moderato. Andante.
                    (Rondo) Allegro.

Pleasant, not profound, the four quartets of op. 8 were
written for members of a Parisian musical establishment
where Stamitz was maître de chapelle; the style is restrained
and the parts simple. Ambivalence toward instrumentation
was prevalent when these were written and there were frequent substitutions such as oboe for flute or clarinet, horn
for viola, or bassoon for cello. Opus 8 no. 1 in D major
is for flute/oboe and strings; no. 2 was originally for oboe,
horn, viola, and bassoon; no. 3 in F major is for oboe/clari-
net and strings; no. 4 in E flat major is for clarinet and
strings.
Parts: Leuckart (Weigelt); McGinnis & Marx (Schuller)

ROSSINI   Quartets, fl, cl, hn, bsn, no. 1, F major;
                    no. 2, G major; no. 3, F major; no. 4, B

flat major; no. 5, D major; no. 6, F major.
Pub. 1829. 10 to 12 min. each. Adv.

Three movement works, the first movements usually
lack a development section and the last are in Rondo form;
they reflect Rossini the opera composer. Even though they
elicit groans sometimes, they are good standby pieces when
the oboe player's out of town. They were originally published
as sonatas, around 1825, for two violins, cello, and double
bass and are still available in that instrumentation from Doblinger in the Diletto Musicale series (251-56). The arrangements for winds were made for Schott by H. Berr in 1829.
Parts: Schott (Zachert) 3164/65

RIISAGER   Quartet, fl, ob, cl, bsn, op. 40a. 1932.
                  14 min. Adv. / Allegro. Andantino.
                  Vivace.

Riisager, a Russian-born Danish composer, writes
here in a modern polyphonic style; crisp, straightforward;
emphasis on rhythm rather than melody. Clarinet part for
A clarinet.
Parts: Dan Fog Musikforlag
Score: Dan Fog Musikforlag

HINDEMITH   Morgenmusik, 2 tpts, 2 trbs. 1932. 8
                  min. Int. / Mässig bewegt. (Lied) Lang-
                  same Viertel. Bewegt.

Hindemith's revival of the sound of medieval "tower
music" was the forerunner and inspiration of many ensembles
written for brass. It was written for and dedicated to amateur musicians at the music festival at Plön. Throughout
there is a good contrapuntal style with tension set up through
the rhythmic and melodic weaving of parts; intervals of
fourths and fifths predominate; trumpets in C; tuba ad libitum.
    Cohn, Europe, 97-98
Parts: Schott 1622
Score: Schott 1622

A. GABRIELI   Ricercar del duodecimo tuono; Ricercar
                  del sesto tuono, 2 tpts, 2 trbs. Pub.
                  1589. 3 min. each. Int.

Andrea Gabrieli's works have been overshadowed by
his famous nephew, Giovanni. In the editorial note of the
Musica Rara edition A. Lumsden notes that these pieces
come from Madrigali e Ricercari a quattro voce published

in Venice in 1589 and are really canzon da sonore in form;
in this edition note values are halved, accidentals added in
accord with modern usage, and dynamics added as editorial
suggestions.   Trumpet parts in B flat; horn may substitute
for second trumpet.
Parts: Musica Rara
Score: Musica Rara

G.   GABRIELI   4 Canzoni per sonare, 2 tpts, 2 trbs.
                     Pub. 1608.   3 min. each.   Int.

     The original collection of 36 canzoni was published in
Venice in 1608 with parts labeled canto, alto, tenore, and
basso.   Musica Rara publishes these four from the 36 as
part of their 20-volume series, Venetian Brass Music of the
Late Sixteenth and Early Seventeenth Centuries.   The Robert
King editions of these four canzoni are published separately;
alternate instrumentations substitute horn and baritone for
trumpet or trombone plus optional tuba.
Parts: Musica Rara; Robert King
Score: Musica Rara; Robert King

BERGSMA   Suite, 2 tpts, bar, trb.   1940.   8 min.
                     Int. / Scherzo.   Song.   Showpiece.

     Three short pieces of moderate difficulty; the opening
Scherzo is crisp, of sparse texture, and intended to sound
rowdy; the second movement is a muted interlude; the third,
whimsically titled, opens with introductory trumpet interplay
on a motif which later alternates with the perky main theme.
     Cobbett, vol. 3, 172
Parts: Fischer
Score: Fischer

---

(4) MIXED QUARTETS

*MOZART   Quartet, ob, vln, vla, vc, K. 368b (370),
                     F major.   1781.   Ded. Friedrich Ramm.
                     16 min.   Adv. / Allegro.   Adagio.   (Ron-
                     do) Allegro.

     The oboe predominates, especially in the fervent Ada-
gio, where the part expresses great intensity and remains in

the upper range of the instrument. Mozart does not relegate
the strings to mere accompaniment--there are many passages
where they weave countermelodies to the oboe. The Rondo
is especially interesting because Mozart writes for the wind
instrument in a different meter than for the strings. Great
technical skill is required of the oboist as well as a high
level of artistry.

Cobbett, vol. 2, 161   King, 15
Einstein, Mozart, 179-
  80
Parts: Boosey; Chester (Rothwell); International; Peters 17B
Score: Boosey; Eulenberg (Peters E194)

*MOZART   Quartet, fl, vln, vla, vc, K. 285, D major.
                 1777. Comm. deJean. 14 min. Int. /
                 Allegro. Adagio. (Rondo) Allegretto.

Even though Mozart did not like to write for flute, he
manages some very beautiful effects here, especially the pizzicato accompaniment of the strings throughout the middle
movement, in imitation of guitar. He does not attempt to
blend the sound of the flute with that of the strings, but allows it to soar above. He was commissioned by deJean to
write three flute quartets, the others being listed as K. 285a,
and K. 285b. A fourth quartet for flute, K. 298, was written
as a parody.
Parts: Breitkopf; Cundy
Parts, collections: International (Rampal); Peters 17A; Schir-
     mer L1836
Score: Bärenreiter TP150 (4 qts); Eulenberg (Peters E192)

HAYDN   Quartet, vln, vla, vc, guitar, Hob. III:8,
                 D major. 20 min. Int. / Allegro.
                 Minuetto alternamente. Adagio. Minuetto
                 alternamente. Presto.

Requires a first-rate guitarist, but the string parts
are easy and can be played by more than one performer to
a part. Haydn scored it for lute--the modern edition prepared for Doblinger by Karl Scheit scores it for guitar. At
one time it was considered a spurious work, until someone
discovered that it was the same as his string quartet op. 2,
no. 2 in E major.
Parts: Bote & Bock; Doblinger

C. P. E. BACH   Quartets, pf, fl, vla, vc, A minor, W.93;
                 D major, W.94, G major, W.95. 1788.
                 12 to 13 min. each. Adv.

Important transitional works with more independent play of parts than was customary at the time this set was conceived--the keyboard part goes far beyond a mere continuo role. Informative notes are given in the score published by Nagels. No cello part was found in the manuscript because in Bach's time it was customary for the publisher to prepare it. The flute part may be played by violin.
Parts: Bärenreiter 2674 (W. 94); Nagels Musik-Archiv 223 (Schmid) (W. 93, W. 95)
Score: Nagels Musik-Archiv 223 (Schmid)

DEVIENNE   Quartet, bsn, vln, vla, vc, op. 73, no. 1, C major. 1780? 12 min. Adv. / Allegro spiritoso. Adagio cantabile.

Devienne was a virtuoso flutist and bassoonist. Notes from the Musica Rara edition tell us that it is one of a set of three quartets for which the manuscripts are lost. The present edition of this work is based on the first edition which came out in Paris toward the end of the 18th century. Devienne also wrote quartets for flute and strings. The bassoon part is quite active in this essentially homophonic setting, but it is woven imaginatively with the string parts, which are never themselves dull. Overall, an enormously pleasing work; the first movement is in tenor clef for the bassoon.
Parts: Musica Rara
Score: Musica Rara (included with parts)

ETLER   Quartet, ob, cl, bsn, vla. 1949. 18 min. Adv. / I. II. III. IV.

Etler is a modern polyphonist, interested in creating tension by juxtaposing linear ideas. As one looks at the score, the viola part does not look any different from the wind parts. The added color of the string seems to be a bonus rather than an inherent aspect. This has audience appeal, sounding "modern" but not "unpleasantly" so. Etler has written a trio scored for oboe, clarinet, and viola called "Sonata" which the players may want to investigate.
Parts: Valley Music Press
Score: Valley Music Press (included with parts)

5 QUINTETS

STRING

*MOZART   Quintet, 2 vlns, 2 vlas, vc, K. 515, C
                 major. 1787. 32 min. Adv. / Allegro.
                 (Menuetto) Allegretto. Andante. Allegro.

With five voices at his disposal, Mozart weaves a
musical fabric that is a marvel of contrapuntal technique;
its musical essence is indescribable--Alfred Einstein feels
that it is a "peerless masterpiece." It opens, distinctively,
with cello alone playing a broad and wide-ranging arpeggio
theme which figures prominently in the dialogue with the violin throughout the movement. The Menuetto has an extraordinary Trio with contrasting sections of its own. K. 515
and its companion, K. 516 in G minor, seem to be the best
known of the quintets. The library should have the set of
six--K. 174, K. 406 (Mozart's arrangement of his Wind Serenade K. 388 in C minor), K. 515, K. 516, K. 593, and K.
614. These are available in two volumes from Peters.
  Cobbett, vol. 2, 162   King, 52-63 (6 qnts)
  Ferguson, 68-69   Landon, 132-34 (6 qnts)
Parts: Breitkopf; Deutscher Verlag
Parts, collections: Kalmus (with K. 516); Peters 18/19
Score: Deutscher Verlag; Eulenberg (Peters E38); Lea 91

*MOZART   Quintet, 2 vlns, 2 vlas, vc, K. 516, G
                 minor. 1787. 34 min. Adv. / Allegro.
                 (Menuetto) Allegretto. Adagio ma non trop-
                 po. Adagio-Allegro.

G minor seems to be Mozart's key of fate, just as
C minor seemed to be Beethoven's. From its very beginning
this quintet has tragic overtones. The Adagio movement is
sublime--Alfred Einstein in his book Mozart describes it as
"the prayer of a lonely one surrounded on all sides by the
walls of a deep chasm." The last movement begins with an

Adagio which gives way, finally, to an Allegro, but one filled
with resignation.   Both this and K. 515 are found in the
Peters volume one.

Cobbett, vol. 2, 162-   King, 52-63 (6 qnts)
64   Landon, 132-34 (6 qnts)
Ferguson, 69-71
Parts: Breitkopf; Kalmus
Parts, collections: Kalmus (with K. 515); Peters 18/19
Score: Eulenberg (Peters E13); Lea 91; Ricordi Pr469

MOZART   Quintet, 2 vlns, 2 vlas, vc, K. 593, D
                major. 1790. 26 min. Adv. / Larghetto-
                Allegro. Adagio. (Menuetto) Allegretto.
                (Finale) Allegro.

Similar in mood to K. 516 in G minor, K. 593 has,
among its distinctive aspects, a dramatic cello part, many
antiphonal passages, and frequent accenting of weak beats.
The first movement opens with an Adagio dialogue between
an ascending arpeggio in the cello and a chorale in the other
strings.   After an Allegro appears and its theme developed,
the Adagio dialogue returns.   The movement ends abruptly
with a brief restatement of the Allegro.   The second movement, tinged with resignation, contains a lovely dialogue between cello and first violin plus antiphonal passages contrasting the two upper strings with the lower.   The Menuetto begins with a lilting, legato theme, offset by the spiccato and
pizzicato effects in its Trio; there is extensive canonic treatment.   In the Finale Mozart leads a sprightly theme of
eighth notes through a series of modulations and contrapuntal
workouts.

Cobbett, vol. 2, 164   King, 52-63 (6 qnts)
Einstein, Mozart, 192-   Landon, 132-34 (6 qnts)
93
Ferguson, 71
Parts: Bärenreiter 4706; Breitkopf; Deutscher Verlag
Parts, collections: Peters 18/19
Score: Bärenreiter TP11; Deutscher Verlag; Eulenberg
(Peters E50)

*SCHUBERT   Quintet, 2 vlns, vla, 2 vcs, op. posth. 163
                (D. 956), C major. Pub. 1853. 45 min.
                Adv. / Allegro ma non troppo. Adagio.
                (Scherzo) Presto-(Trio) Andante sostenuto.
                Allegretto.

An all-time favorite, and not only of cellists.   In the
Allegro the two cellos in duet introduce the secondary theme.

The exquisite Adagio begins with organ-like sonorities accompanied by dramatic pizzicati--its calm is interrupted suddenly by agitated movement from the cellos which subsides gradually; as the calm returns, the lower cello continues a rumbling undercurrent on its own. The Scherzo has an unusual Trio in 4/4 meter which is an elegaic folk hymn, its declamatory style in great contrast to the dance character of the movement opening. The last movement is dance-like and offers the players many opportunities for virtuoso spiccato playing.

Cobbett, vol. 2, 362-64   Laciar, 533-37

Einstein, Schubert,   Robertson, 167-74
290-92   Westrup, 18-22

Ferguson, 149-53

Parts: Breitkopf; International; Peters 775
Score: Boosey 284; Eulenberg (Peters E15); Universal Edition Ph375

*BRAHMS   Quintet, 2 vlns, 2 vlas, vc, op. 88, F
                 major, "Spring." 1882. 26 min. Adv.   /
                 Allegro non troppo ma con brio. Grave ed
                 appassionato-Allegretto vivace. Allegro
                 energico.

Opus 88 is less complicated rhythmically and harmonically than op. 111, its companion string quintet, which makes it easier for players to cope with. The first movement, with its broad theme and hopping rhythm, is most attractive; its second combines a Grave theme with two lighthearted episodes, creating a Rondo effect; the final movement is built on a fugue in 3/2 meter with a subject of a long staccato eighth-note pattern--some legato relief appears midway in the movement and about 40 bars from the end a Presto in 9/8 meter appears to bring down the final curtain.

Cobbett, vol. 1, 177   Ferguson, 207-8
Colles, 46-48   Keys, 26-28
Drinker, 84-86   Mason, Brahms, 149-59
Evans, vol. 2, 104-20

Parts: International; Kalmus; Peters 3905A
Score: Eulenberg (Peters E237); Kalmus; Lea 169 (with op. 111, op. 115); Peters (Brahms Chamber Music, vol. 1)

BRAHMS   Quintet, 2 vlns, 2 vlas, vc, op. 111, G
                 major. Pub. 1891. 26 min. Adv.   /
                 Allegro non troppo, ma con brio. Adagio.
                 Un poco allegretto. Vivace ma non troppo
                 presto.

Of Brahms' two string quintets, this, the more mature work, is also the more inspired. Upon its completion, Brahms thought his creative life had come to an end. Its first two movements are rather complex, with great rhythmic independence of the parts; the cello solo at the opening requires the utmost projection because Brahms intended the accompanying parts to sound full. The Adagio is gorgeous, made more so by the contrast of pizzicato against the legato theme; at its close, the solo viola is favored with a cadenza. Although op. 88 is called the "Spring" quintet, the third movement of this quintet, a simple dance, is the quintessence of spring. The last movement is typically energetic, ending with a favorite of Brahms, the Hungarian Czardas.

Cobbett, vol. 1, 179-80   Ferguson, 208-10
Colles, 54-57   Keys, 28-30
Drinker, 92-95   Mason, Brahms, 202-18
Evans, vol. 2, 243-62

Parts: International; Kalmus; Peters 3905B
Score: Eulenberg (Peters E238); Lea 169 (with op. 88, op. 115); Peters (Brahms Chamber Music, vol. 1)

DVOŘÁK   Quintet, 2 vlns, vla, vc, dbl bass, op. 77 (B. 49), G major. 1875. Ded. "To My Nation." 33 min. Adv. / Allegro con fuoco. (Scherzo) Allegro vivace. Poco andante. (Finale) Allegro assai.

This quintet is given priority here to op. 97, the more popular quintet, because it seems more interesting musically, it offers additional repertoire to the double-bass players, and is less likely to be owned by string players. The cello part roams more freely, relieved of its usual duties as the lowest instrument. Except for the broad flow of the third movement, the themes are short and dance-like; the last movement is a rollicking one.

Sourek, 33-37
Parts: Artia; International; Simrock
Score: Artia; Eulenberg (Peters E338)

DVOŘÁK   Quintet, 2 vlns, 2 vlas, vc, op. 97 (B. 180), E flat major. 1893. 30 min. Adv. / Allegro non tanto. Allegro vivo. Larghetto. (Finale) Allegro giusto.

This opus has the flavor of the "New World" Symphony, with its hopping rhythms reminiscent of Indian drums and

pentatonic melodies imitating Indian melodies. It makes a
good companion piece to the Brahms and Mozart quintets.
Cobbett, vol. 1, 362-   Sourek, 37-44
63
Parts: Artia; International; Simrock
Score: Artia; Eulenberg (Peters E306)

BOCCHERINI   Quintet, 2 vlns, 2 vlas, vc, op. 60, no. 5
(G. 395), G major. 1801. Ded. Lucien
Bonaparte. 18 min. Adv. / Allegro con
moto. (Minuetto) Allegro risoluto. Andantino. Allegro giusto.

Boccherini wrote innumerable string quintets, many of
them discovered and published years after his death. He
was a prolific writer--attribution and numbering have always
been difficult. Gérard's catalogue will be an enormous aid
in systematizing publishing numbers. The dedication of this
work was to an amateur cellist, a French diplomat in Spain
who was a relative of Napoleon's. The music is monothematic, with many motifs within each movement. There are 12
two-viola quintets available as separates through Doblinger.
Parts: Doblinger (Sabatini)

BOCCHERINI   Quintet, 2 vlns, vla, 2 vcs, G. 378, C
major. 18 min. Adv. / Andante con
moto. Minuet. Grave. Rondo.

This is more representative of Boccherini, inasmuch
as he favored quintets with two cellos; the cello parts are
difficult at times, especially the solo part, which is usually
in the higher register. This quintet is a very special one
because it is a "scissors and paste" job--the Andante is
from G. 349, the Minuet from G. 314, the Grave from G.
325, and the Rondo from G. 310. A bargain on anyone's
terms! Happily, it comes off as a unified whole. The larger
library may want the Ricordi edition in three volumes, which
includes six other two-cello quintets, G. 275, G. 280, G.
377, G. 339, G. 300, and G. 376.
Parts: International (Lauterbach); Peters (Lauterbach)
Parts, collections: Ricordi ER2171/73/75

BRUCKNER   Quintet, 2 vlns, 2 vlas, vc, F major. 1879.
Ded. Max Emanuel. 40 min. Adv. /
Gemässigt, Moderato. (Scherzo) Schnell-
Langsam. Adagio. (Finale) Lebhaft bewegt.

Bruckner's only contribution to chamber music is not

a miniature symphony, as one might expect, but an authentic example of the genre.   It is romantic and lengthy, with typical Brucknerian key shifts, long pedal points, broad themes, and sameness of mood throughout.   The Adagio (in six flats) is prayerful in mood but intricately structured in polyphonic style.   Bruckner makes effective use of a motif which is presented first in descending form and then used in contrary motion to its inversion and is also treated fugally.   The quintet was requested around 1861 by a well-known quartet leader, but by 1879 when it was finally complete, Bruckner's style had changed so much that it was unacceptable to the leader, especially the Scherzo.   Bruckner wrote an Intermezzo in its place which is available from International, published as a separate.

    Cobbett, vol. 1, 215-16   Redlich, 253-58
Parts: Breitkopf; Bruckner Verlag (Peters BR47) (inc. Inter-
    mezzo); International (Intermezzo separate); Peters 3842
Score: Bruckner Verlag (Peters BR41) (with Intermezzo);
    Eulenberg (Peters E310); Universal Edition Ph213

---

(5) PIANO QUINTETS

*SCHUMANN   Quintet, piano, op. 44, E flat major.   Pub.
                1843.   32 min.   Adv.   /   Allegro brillante.
                In modo d'una Marcia.   Un poco largamente.
                Scherzo molto vivace.   Allegro ma non trop-
                po.

    Schumann at his best; one of the most celebrated works in the literature which remains fresh.   Appropriate to the quintet is Donald Francis Tovey's remark in Essays in Musical Analysis (p. 150) that "Schumann is a delightfully epigrammatic composer with a great power of making very simple things tell."   If the players exercise restraint, the exuberance inherent in the work will not become forced--the pianist has to make a special effort to blend with the strings. The first movement begins energetically with the piano presenting the initial theme and the cello introducing the broad, lyrical secondary theme.   The second movement is a mournful melody punctuated by short heavy beats mindful of foot steps in a dirge--it is interrupted twice, first by an ethereal interlude and then by an impassioned one.   The Scherzo is dominated by rushing scales--the speed and the placement of accents may be problematic.   The two contrasting trios of the Scherzo (in simple duple meter as contrasted to the opening 6/8 meter) move through many key regions. The last movement contains a remarkable fugue which combines the Finale theme with the initial theme of the first movement.

Cobbett, vol. 2, 379-82   Tovey, Chamber Music, 149-54

Ferguson, 170-71

Parts: Augener 7166; Breitkopf; International; Peters 2381; Schirmer L1648

Score: Eulenberg (Peters E78); Ricordi Pr463

*BRAHMS   Quintet, piano, op. 34, F minor. Pub. 1865. Ded. Princess Anna of Hesse. 40 min. Adv. / Allegro non troppo. Andante, un poco adagio. (Scherzo) Allegro. (Finale) Poco sostenuto.

A musical feast for devotees of Brahms. One of his most representative compositions, rich in musical ideas that are brilliantly developed. Every movement invites structural analysis. Before it became a piano quintet, Brahms had tried it as a string quintet and as a piano duet. With the exception of the tender second movement, the work can be characterized as one that is tightly knit structurally, with dramatic shifts of mood and intense rhythmic vigor. One of the most dramatic shifts is in the Scherzo, which rises from an ominous opening to a heroic theme. The Scherzo also contains a marvelous fugue passage near the end; driving reiterated rhythmic figures bring the movement to a ferocious close.

Cobbett, vol. 1, 170   Ferguson, 198-201
Drinker, 100-106   Keys, 8-14
Evans, vol. 1, 137-58   Mason, Brahms, 43-54

Parts: Breitkopf; International; Peters 3660; Schirmer L1646

Score: Eulenberg (Peters E212); Heugel Ph188; Peters; Ricordi Pr483

DVOŘÁK   Quintet, piano, op. 81 (B. 155), A major. 1887. Ded. Professor Neureutter. 32 min. Adv. / Allegro ma non tanto. (Dumka) Andante con moto. (Scherzo) Molto vivace. (Finale) Allegro.

The cellist and the violist will appreciate their soloistic roles and Dvořák's even distribution of thematic material, which is often parceled out in four-measure phrases for piano alternating with four-measure phrases for strings. The viola

plays a prominent role in the Dumka movement. The mood
of the quintet is generally exuberant--paradoxically, there
is a melancholic strain in every movement. The Dumka,
in particular, demonstrates this contrast--it is a richly inventive set of variations on a meditative theme. Throughout
the work there are many different rhythms going on simul-
taneously, and many accidentals in the parts. The Scherzo
movement is brilliant, as is the last, which contains a
challenging fugue passage near the end. The piano part is
brilliant but instead of dominating, the pianism works for
the overall good of the ensemble.
        Cobbett, vol. 1, 366-   Sourek, 50-56
          68
        Ferguson, 232-33
Parts: Artia; International; Simrock
Score: Artia; Eulenberg (Peters E305)

FRANCK   Quintet, piano, F minor. 1878. 32 min.
                    Adv. /   Molto moderato quasi lento-Allegro.
                    Lento, con moto sentimento. Allegro non
                    troppo, ma con fuoco.

        The cyclic form used by Franck combines and trans-
forms motifs in a variety of ways and allows them to reappear
in each movement. The appeal of the quintet is not immediate; however, players may profit from experiencing a melodic and textural style they are less familiar with; the style
is typified by repetitious fragments of melody, lengthy passages in unison, or the same rhythm appearing in all parts.
The first movement opens dramatically with impassioned
strings alternating with tender statements from the piano,
which eventually leads the transition to the Allegro section.
The second movement is tranquil, the third opening with a
perpetual motion figure on a short rising chromatic sequence
which, begun by violin alone, is taken up by all in turn
against the broad theme presented in the piano part--the piano
part assumes the perpetual motion figure while the strings
sing out the broad theme.
        Cobbett, vol. 1, 422-   Robertson, 365-68
          24
        Ferguson, 245-46
Parts: Hamelle; International; Peters 3743
Score: no information available

SHOSTAKOVICH   Quintet, piano, op. 57, G minor. 1940.
                    38 min. Adv. /   (Prelude) Lento.
                    (Fugue) Adagio. (Scherzo) Allegretto.
                    (Intermezzo) Lento. (Finale) Allegretto.

Considered one of the best works of the composer;
demonstrates his particular adaptation of classical polyphonic
principles. The mood is sustained and lyrical. The opening
of the Fugue movement is distinctive as the violin, muted,
begins a sad Russian song, joined first by the other strings
and then by piano. The Intermezzo is dominated by solo
violin, at first accompanied by cello pizzicato and later joined
by the others in a marvelous weaving of voices. The Finale
establishes a tranquil mood.

Cobbett, vol. 3, 144   Robertson, 420-21
Martynov, 89-100
Parts: International; Music Corporation of America; Peters
    4791
Score: International

BERWALD   Quintet, piano, no. 1, op. 5, C minor.
               1853. Ded. Hilda Thegerström. 25 min.
               Adv. / Allegro molto. Scherzo poco al-
               legretto. Adagio quasi andante. Allegro
               assai e con spiritoso.

A Swedish composer of German origin who spent most
of his life in Germany, Franz Berwald received little recognition for what turned out to be originality, outside the ad-
miration of a few "lights" such as Franz Liszt and Richard
Wagner. However, during the last decade or so, his name
has been steadily rising out of this undeserved obscurity.
The prestigious firm of Bärenreiter plans to publish all his
works. This quintet, the first of two, is considered the
more inventive one. Present-day listeners will find it charming and full of subtle humor. A biography is available,
Franz Berwald by Robert Layton (London: Anthony Blond,
1959).

Cobbett, vol. 1, 125
Parts: Gehrmans

FINNEY   Quintet, piano. 1953. 23 min. Adv. /
               Adagio sostenuto-Allegro marcato. Allegro
               scherzando. Nocturne. Allegro appassionata.

Contemporary piano quintets such as this and the Walter Piston (1949) offer interesting and fresh contrasts to the
standard romantic repertoire. Finney's is a dodecaphonic
work of moderate difficulty in which he claims to use a free
approach to tone rows. The first movement he describes as
a fantasy, the second as a modified rondo, the third as a
nocturne, and the fourth as a three-part unit (ABC) which is
developed and recapitulated.

Cobbett, vol. 3, 171
Parts: Peters 6457

---

(5) WIND QUINTETS

*HINDEMITH   Kleine Kammermusik (Little Chamber Music),
                    fl, ob, cl, hn, bsn, op. 24, no. 2. 1922.
                    14 min. Adv. / Lustig, Mässig schnelle
                    Viertel. (Walzer) Durchweg sehr leise.
                    Ruhig und einfach, Achtel. Schnelle Viertel.
                    Sehr lebhaft.

        If there were to be one woodwind quintet in a library,
it would have to be this--music perfectly suited to winds;
idiomatic writing at its best.   When most other compositions
by Hindemith are forgotten, this will continue to hold its
place in the repertoire. There are several recordings available. Difficulties for the players lie in the rhythmic aspects
--tempo changes and shifting meters and accents. Flute
player doubles on piccolo.
        Cobbett, vol. 1, 559-   Robertson, 315
            60
        Cohn, Europe, 114
Parts: Associated Music Publishers; Schott 4389
Score: Schott 3437

MILHAUD   La Cheminée du roi René (The Chimney of
                    King René), suite, fl, ob, cl, hn, bsn.
                    1939. 18 min. Adv. / Cortège. Aubade
                    [Morning Serenade]. Jongleurs [Jugglers].
                    La Maousinglade. Joutes sur l'arc [Jousts
                    on the Arc]. Chasse à Valabre [Hunting at
                    Valabre]. Madrigal-Nocturne.

        René was a beloved 15th-century king of Provence.
Milhaud, who was born in Provence, evokes the spirit of
medieval times, externally in his choice of titles and inter-
nally in his choice of scales and intervals which call to mind
the music of that time. He makes the most of the color resources or timbres of the winds. Each part is interesting
to play. Flute player doubles on piccolo. The title of this
piece refers to a favorite sunny spot of the King's, where he
walked each day.
        Cohn, Europe, 217

Parts: Southern Music (Texas)
Score: Southern Music (Texas)

IBERT   Trois pièces brèves, fl, ob, cl, hn, bsn.
                   Pub. 1930. 9 min. Adv. / Allegro.
                   Andante. Assez lent.

     These pieces have become so popular that they are
suffering from over-exposure; light and frothy, they show
off the resources of the winds. The last movement is circus
music, with the clarinet in center ring.
     Cohn, Europe, 142
Parts: Leduc
Score: Leduc

NIELSEN   Quintet, fl, ob, cl, hn, bsn, op. 43. Pub.
                   1923. 24 min. Adv. / Allegro ben mod-
                   erato. Menuet. Praeludium-Adagio-Tema
                   con variazioni-Un poco andantino.

     A popular piece among wind players which Peters, in
Literature of the Woodwind Quintet, characterizes as conser-
vative and neo-romantic. Nielsen wrote it for members of
the Copenhagen Wind Quintet whom he knew personally and
styled the parts to fit the personalities of the players. The
first movement is broad and relaxed, combining a flowing
theme with a staccato one; flute and clarinet have interesting
figurations. The last movement is multi-sectional, with a
dark, sombre English horn solo at the opening; the instruments
are featured individually in the variations; there is a chorale
close. Difficulties for the players may be caused by virtuoso-
like passages with unusual fingering patterns which arise from
the harmonic relationships, and faulty intonation. Oboe player
doubles on English horn; clarinet in A.
     Peters, 87   Robertson, 313-14
Parts: Hansen Nr2285B
Score: Hansen; Musica Rara

FINE   Partita, fl, ob, cl, hn, bsn. 1948. 14
                   min. Adv. / (Introduction and Theme)
                   Allegro moderato. (Variation) Poco vivace.
                   (Interlude) Adagio. (Gigue) Allegro. (Coda)
                   Lento assai.

     A first-rate composition with "motor" vitality; Fine
does not seek to take advantage of the tonal resources at his
disposal, but rather aims at a polyphonic texture of disjunct
fragments that does not require distinctions of timbre. The

result could be described as dry, crisp, or clear-cut. Meter changes are frequent; however the speed of the eighth note remains the same. The final movement is a very slow coda which provides great contrast to the preceding Gigue. The Gigue itself can be taxing to play, especially for the horn player.

Cobbett, vol. 3, 171-
72

Parts: Boosey
Score: Boosey

Cohn, Western Hemi-
sphere, 95

ETLER   Quintet, fl, ob, cl, hn, bsn, no. 1. 1955.
               Ded. New York Wind Quintet. 16 min.
               Adv. / Andante. Allegro. Lento. Vi-
               vace.

Contrapuntal in style and similar to Fine's Partita in that the focus is on movement of parts rather than on instrumental color; Etler is economical--many times there are only two voices sounding. It is not difficult, but may sound difficult, which pleases performers. Etler's second woodwind quintet (1957) is a good work, also; however, it is thicker in texture and somewhat more complex.

Peters, 54
Parts: Associated Music Publishers
Score: Associated Music Publishers

PERSICHETTI   Pastoral, fl, ob, cl, hn, bsn, op. 21. 1945.
               9 min. Int.

Another neo-classicist; a good opening piece for a program, or for an intermediate-level ensemble. The piece opens with a melodic motif presented by the flute in a moderate tempo; later, the clarinet joins with a counter-melody. Halfway through, the character changes from a legato style to a brisker, jauntier one, all the while developing the fragmentary theme first presented by the flute. Frequent changes of meter.

Cobbett, vol. 3, 172
Parts: Schirmer
Score: Schirmer

VOXMAN   Ensemble Repertoire for Woodwind Quintet.
               1960. Int.

The duration of pieces in the collection varies; excellent material for the neophyte; well chosen and tastefully arranged. Voxman has arranged pieces for other wind combina-

tions such as two clarinets, flute and clarinet, etc. which
are excellent and inexpensive; parts often come in score form.
Parts: Rubank

ANDRAUD   Twenty-Two Woodwind Quintets.   Int. -Adv.

This collection has been around for over 25 years and
is still the "stand-by" collection.   At least one in every five
players owns it.   About half the collection is original material, the rest is arrangements or pieces for trios and quartets.
It includes the fairly well known quintet by Paul Taffanel and
an arrangement of Beethoven's op. 71.
Parts: Southern Music (Texas)

REICHA   Quintet, fl, ob, cl, hn, bsn, op. 88, no.
                 2, E flat major.   25 min.   Adv. / Lento-
                 Allegro moderato.   (Scherzo) Allegro.   An-
                 dante grazioso.   (Finale) Allegro molto.

There are about two dozen Reicha quintets in publication; op. 88 contains six and there are also six each in op.
91, op. 99, and op. 100.   The library should have some examples of these "classical" quintets; movements are rapid
enough to challenge the best players of today and cause ad-
miration for the players of Reicha's time who had inferior
instruments compared to today's, at least in terms of mecha-
nism.
Parts: Leuckart (Weigelt); Musica Rara; WIM (Wise)

SCHOENBERG   Quintet, fl, ob, cl, hn, bsn, op. 26.   1924.
                 Ded. Bubi Arnold.   40 min.   Adv. + /
                 Schwungvoll.   Anmutig und heiter, scher-
                 zando.   Etwas langsam.   Rondo.

Excluding avant-garde, this may be the most difficult
quintet in the repertoire, not necessarily from a technical
standpoint as from a conceptual one.   Felix Greissle indicates
in his notes for the Universal-Edition score that this is the
first large work in which Schoenberg substantiated the laws
of composition with 12 tones.   Structurally, it follows traditional patterns, the first movement in sonata-allegro form
and the last in rondo form.   Schoenberg gives some guidance
to the players in his carefully annotated score; he indicates
primary and secondary themes as well as types of accents
desired.   The library, in purchasing parts for significant
works such as this, will help to overcome neglect and preju-
dice by giving players an opportunity to examine works they
might never purchase.   Flute doubles on piccolo.

Cohn, <u>Europe</u>, 267-68   Whittall, 36-42
Robertson, 312
Parts: Belmont
Score: Belmont

CARTER   Quintet, fl, ob, cl, hn, bsn. 1948. 10
                min. Adv. / Allegretto. Allegro giocoso.

Carter is a very significant American composer, some
of whose works are rarely performed because they are quite
difficult. This work is not as difficult for wind players as
his string quartets are for string players, hence it was
chosen to represent Carter in this guide. It is complex
harmonically; the second movement is built on a dance
rhythm--it requires a high degree of tonguing proficiency; the
results can be dazzling.
Parts: Associated Music Publishers
Score: Associated Music Publishers

BADINGS   Quintet, fl, ob, cl, hn, bsn. 1949. 12 min.
                 Adv. / Allegro. Adagio. Allegro.

A solid, well-organized piece to which players respond
favorably. Parts are rhythmically independent; there is much
dovetailing. Outer movements are perky--in the first, the
theme, a descending motif, is worked out and passed around;
the last changes pace several times, alternating fast with
tranquil sections. The melodic line of the Adagio remains
within a narrow interval range, with major or minor seconds
predominating.
Cobbett, vol. 3, 79, 80
Parts: Donemus
Score: no information available

DANZI   Quintet, fl, ob, cl, hn, bsn, op. 56, no. 2,
               G minor. Pub. 1914 (1st modern edition).
               15 min. Adv. / Allegretto. Andante.
               (Minuetto) Allegretto. Allegretto.

Danzi's musical training was of the Mannheim School
and his numerous quintets exemplify the casual divertimento
style of wind music at that time. There is grace and refinement, but a general lack of depth. Movements are suite-
like with frequent solo passages and challenging sections of
rapid staccato. Op. 56, no. 2 is quite well known and was
the first Danzi to appear in a modern edition (Breitkopf &
Härtel, 1914). Another well known one, slightly more difficult, is op. 68, no. 3 in D minor. Publishing information
for several of the quintets is given below.

Parts: Associated Music Publishers (op. 56, no. 1, no. 2);
Leuckart (op. 56, no. 1, no. 2, no. 3; op. 67, no. 1);
McGinnis & Marx (op. 56, no. 1, no. 2); Musica Rara
(op. 56, no. 1, no. 2; op. 68, no. 3; op. 76, no. 2);
Peters (op. 67, no. 2, no. 3; op. 68, no. 2)
Score: no information available

COWELL   Suite, fl, ob, cl, hn, bsn. 1949. 8 min.
                Adv. / Allegretto. Allegro. Adagio can-
                tabile. Allegretto con moto.

Each of the brief movements ends with a saucy dissonance; the suite begins with a little theme and a busy, rippling accompaniment which are passed around; a perky theme
in perpetual motion and a chorale comprise the inner movements; the last is a pulsating fugato in a clipped style.
Parts: Presser
Score: no information available

SCHULLER   Suite, fl, ob, cl, hn, bsn. 1958. 18 min.
                Adv. / (Prelude) Allegro. (Blues) An-
                dante. (Toccata) Presto.

Inconsequential but popular. The Prelude, characterized by quartal harmony, has a contrasting misterioso middle
section in a fugato style, where the interval of a fourth becomes important melodically; each instrument has a cell group
of notes which is varied rhythmically. Of interest in the
second movement, which is a banal 12-bar blues, is the attempt to notate jazz phrasing. The Toccata is another rhythmic play on a group of cell notes for each instrument--the
oboe part is the only one with a key signature (B minor) and
carries the legato theme above the reiterated rhythms of the
other parts.
Parts: McGinnis & Marx
Score: McGinnis & Marx

FRANÇAIX   Quintet, fl, ob, cl, hn, bsn. 1949. Ded.
                Quintette à vent de l'Orchestre National de
                Paris. 19 min. Adv. / Andante tran-
                quillo-Allegro assai. Presto. Tema-
                Variations. Tempo di marcia francese.

A sparkling tour-de-force which skims along propulsive-
ly, always avoiding the ponderous. Françaix uses melodic
and harmonic elements in such a way as to give certain sections of each movement a percussive cast. He frequently
uses perpetual motion figures and likes to support plaintive

melodies with rollicking accompaniments. Many portions have the sequential harmonic flavor of 1920s jazz. Challenges to the players in key signatures, awkward interval patterns in perpetual motion figures and rapid articulations. The opening Andante features a legato horn solo with a wide interval range; the bassoon part is full of leaping intervals. Clarinet part for A clarinet.

Parts: Schott 4121
Score: Schott 4103

VALEN   Serenade, fl, ob, cl, hn, bsn, op. 42.
                    1947. 8 min. Adv. / Allegro moderato.

        Valen intended to write a woodwind quintet for a Danish group but completed only this movement, which is in a very subdued mood. Valen's music, although 12-tone based, is unlike that of the Viennese school. It is based on an elaboration of motifs rather than a tone row. This somber work does not have immediate appeal. There is a good analysis in the Kortsen and a recording available on the Philips label (839-248AY).
        Kortsen, Contemporary
            Norwegian, 221-25
Parts: H. Lyche
Score: H. Lyche

PEZEL   Five Part Brass Music, 2 tpts, hn, 2 trbs.
                    Pub. 1685. 2 min. each. Int.

        The Musica Rara edition of these 76 pieces is based on the 1685 part books. The collection, edited by A. Lumsden and available in three volumes, has been transposed down a step to be nearer the original sound. The text is free of phrasing; dynamics are editorial suggestions. Pezel was the town band leader in Leipzig--the town band played for all official ceremonies. The collection contains "... Intradas, Allemandes, Ballets, Courantes, Sarabandes, and Gigues... "; horn part may be played by trombone. Robert King has also published several of the pieces. Pezel's Sonatas from Hora Decima (1670) are also available from Musica Rara (two volumes) and from Robert King and Boosey & Hawkes.
Parts: King (separates: Six Pieces; Three Pieces); Musica
        Rara (complete, 3 vols.)
Score: King (separates: Six Pieces; Three Pieces); Musica
        Rara (complete, 3 vols.)

HOLBORNE   Complete Music for Brass, 2 tpts, hn, 2
                    trbs. 1599. 3 to 5 min. each. Int.

Holborne was a lutenist, a poet, and a courtier to
Queen Elizabeth I. The collection is entitled Pavans, Gal-
liards, Almains, and other Short Aeirs both Grave and Light
in Five Parts for Viols, Violins, or other Musical Wind Instruments. It is available in two volumes from Musica Rara
with helpful notes on the editing, and an article by L. Kot-
tick on phrasing, articulation, and accent in Renaissance
music. Robert King, who pioneered editing of early brass
music, has published Five Pieces from the collection. Alternate instrumentations: 2 tpts, hn/trb, trb/hn, baritone/
trb, tuba optional. Associated Music Publishers has published some of the collection as Suite of Elizabethan Dances,
arranged by G. Schwarz.
Parts: Associated Music Publishers (Schwarz); King (Five
    Pieces); Musica Rara (complete, 2 vols.)
Score: Associated Music Publishers (Schwarz); King (Five
    Pieces); Musica Rara (complete, 2 vols.)

SANDERS   Quintet, 2 tpts, hn, 2 trbs, B flat major.
                1942. 15 min. Adv. / Grave-Allegro.
                Adagio. Allegro vivo.

In a conventional "Hindemith" style and of moderate
difficulty, this quintet is described in Brass Quarterly (June,
1958) as "in a true chamber music style" and "unusually
grateful" as well as "well-written." Trumpet parts may be
played by cornets, trombone parts by baritones.
Parts: Fischer; King; Mercury
Score: Fischer; King

DAHL   Music for Brass Instruments, 2 tpts, hn,
                2 trbs. 1944. Ded. Gail Kubik. 15 min.
                Adv. + / (Chorale Fantasy on "Christ Lay
                in the Bonds of Death") Sostenuto. (Inter-
                mezzo) Allegro leggiero. (Fugue) Moderato.

A unique, challenging work which is free of the "tower
music" sound; good idiomatic writing. The Intermezzo offers
a crisp and syncopated contrast to the Chorale Fantasy.
Trumpet parts in B flat; tuba part ad libitum.
Parts: Witmark
Score: Witmark

ETLER   Quintet, 2 tpts, hn, trb, tuba. 1963. 15
                min. Adv. + / I. II. III. IV.

Displays Etler's characteristic clarity and refinement;
a great deal of color is drawn from the five brasses through

voicings and special effects such as glissando, muting, half
valve, flutter tonguing, trills, and juxtapositions of staccato
and legato.   Obviously influenced by the variety of instrumental tone color brought forth in the works of Bartók and
Schoenberg; obviously conversant with jazz band techniques.
Individual parts are quite independent.   The last movement
is remarkable for its unrelenting rhythmic drive.   Trumpet
parts in B flat.
Parts: Associated Music Publishers
Score: Associated Music Publishers

SCHULLER   Quintet, 2 tpts, hn, trb, tuba.   1961.   Comm.
                  Library of Congress.   12 min.   Adv. +

    The use of straightforward brass and pointillistic
ideas suggests the Webern Concerto; the various attacks, the
registrations, and the timbre mixes are a translation of
Schoenberg's varying string color into the brass realm; scraps
and references here and there to the composer's peripheral
jazz experience; a kaleidoscope of timbre mixes.
Parts: Associated Music Publishers
Score: Associated Music Publishers

---

(5) MIXED QUINTETS

*SCHUBERT   Quintet, pf, vln, vla, vc, dbl bass, op.
                  posth.   114 (D. 667), A major, "Trout."
                  1829.   38 min.   Adv. /   Allegro vivace.
                  Andante.   (Scherzo) Presto.   (Tema) An-
                  dantino.   (Finale) Allegro giusto.

    The "Trout" quintet is widely known.   The theme of
the fourth movement is that of Schubert's song "Die Forelle"
or "The Trout."   The piano part is written in a higher than
usual range to accommodate the independence of the double
bass.   Also, the piano part frequently consists of octave
doublings.   Typical Schubert clarity of texture and frequent
shifts of tonality are present.   The Andante is uniquely organized, tonally--three themes, one in F major, one in F
sharp minor, and one in D major, are each presented twice,
but the second presentation is in a key a minor third above
the first.   This makes a dramatic effect as well as an original and effective way to return to the key in which the movement opens.

Cobbett, vol. 2, 356-   Robertson, 146-52
    57   Westrup, 6-13
Einstein, Schubert,
    158-59
Ferguson, 139-41
Parts: Breitkopf; International; Peters 169
Score: Boosey 185; Eulenberg (Peters E118); Universal Edition 475

*MOZART   Quintet, cl, 2 vlns, vla, vc, K. 581, A
                 major, "Stadler." 1789. 28 min. Adv. ∕
                 Allegro. Larghetto. Menuetto. Allegretto
                 con variazioni.

A masterpiece of the literature in which fortune
smiled on clarinet players; it is very well known in general
music circles and recordings are relatively abundant; there
are frequent performances. It is not soloistic in style,
rather it displays a perfect balance of motivic materials and
timbres. The Larghetto is reminiscent of the Adagio from
the Mozart Clarinet Concerto. In this movement, the clarinet and first violin weave the melodic thread while the other
instruments contribute a "sotto voce" accompaniment. Clarinet in A.
    Cobbett, vol. 2, 165   Ferguson, 72-73
    Einstein, Mozart, 194-   Robertson, 89
    95
Parts: Boosey; Breitkopf; International; Peters 19A
Score: Boosey; Eulenberg (Peters E71)

*MOZART   Quintet, pf, ob, cl, hn, bsn, K. 452, E
                 flat major. 1784. 22 min. Adv. ∕ Lar-
                 go-Allegro moderato. Larghetto. (Rondo)
                 Allegretto.

A stroke of fortune for wind players that Mozart
turned his genius to this combination and that Beethoven chose
to imitate it. Mozart's genius for balance is evident--the
piano never dominates and there is alternation between piano
sound and wind sound. The phrases are adapted to the breath
requirements of the performers. The last movement contains a unique concerted cadenza for all the winds, taking up
47 bars near the close. The work makes musical rather
than technical demands; players will need to develop a uni-
formity of approach to the phrasing and ornamentation.
    Cobbett, vol. 2, 167   Tovey, Chamber Music,
    Robertson, 293-96   106-20

Parts: Breitkopf; International; Musica Rara; Peters
Score: International

*BEETHOVEN   Quintet, pf, ob, cl, hn, bsn, op. 16, E
               flat major. 1796. Ded. Joseph Schwartzen-
               berg. 25 min. Adv. / Grave-Allegro
               ma non troppo. Andante cantabile. (Rondo)
               Allegro ma non troppo.

     Modeled after Mozart's K. 452, it is not quite equal
to it in balance or inventiveness. The piano part dominates
more; wind players have long stretches without piano. The
slow introduction in the first movements of both the Mozart
and the Beethoven pose problems of intonation, agreement
on the duration of long notes, and keeping the tempo moving
forward instead of slowing down.
     Robertson, 299-302   Tovey, Chamber Music,
     Scherman, 156-57   106-20
Parts: Breitkopf; International; Musica Rara; Peters
Score: International

*BRAHMS   Quintet, cl, 2 vlns, vla, vc, op. 115, B
               minor. Pub. 1892. 40 min. Adv. /
               Allegro. Adagio. Andantino. Presto no
               assai, ma con sentimento. Con moto-Un
               poco meno mosso.

     A real challenge to string players because of its
orchestral texture and complex rhythms; string players often
become so involved with intonation and fingering problems
that balance and tone suffer. In general, the clarinet functions as a string instrument in regard to the thematic material given to it and its place in the weave of the musical fabric; however, in the Adagio the clarinet is the solo voice,
with opportunities to rhapsodize over muted, subdued strings.
This Adagio is one of the dramatic high points in the clarinet
literature. Clarinet in A; a viola may substitute for clarinet--
a viola part is usually furnished by the publisher.
     Cobbett, vol. 1, 180-81   Evans, vol. 2, 282-303
     Colles, 59-62   Ferguson, 210-12
     Drinker, 127-30   Keys, 62-66
Parts: Boosey; Breitkopf; International; Peters
Score: Boosey; Eulenberg (Peters E239); Ricordi Pr482

BOCCHERINI   Quintet, 2 vlns, vla, vc, guitar, G. 448, D
               major. 19 min. Adv. / Allegro maestoso.
               Pastorale. Grave assai-Fandango.

The composer transcribed this quintet from some of
his other works.   There are some unusual effects throughout,
e. g. , in the Fandango, there are Spanish rhythms and melodies, while in the Pastorale there are effects such as trills
which somehow convey a bucolic scene, replete with birds.
Several other guitar quintets are available--G. 453 in C
major and G. 451 in E minor.
Parts: Peters ZM1044
Score: Heugel (with 5 guitar quintets)

MOZART   Quintet, hn, vln, 2 vlas, vc, K. 386c (407),
                    E flat major. 1782. Ded. Ignaz Leutgeb.
                    16 min. Adv. / Allegro. Andante. Al-
                    legro.

A virtuoso horn part and minor string parts make this
a miniature horn concerto.   The horn part is a singing one,
full of good humor.   Sometimes a violin is substituted for a
horn and publishers such as Peters include the piece in volumes for string quintets.   Mozart uses two violas instead of
two violins for the sake of tonal color and balance with the horn.
      Cobbett, vol. 2, 165   King, 15-16
      Einstein, Mozart, 194
Parts: Breitkopf; International; Peters 19D
Parts, collections: Peters 18/19 (vol. 2 contains K. 407)
Score: Deutscher Verlag; Eulenberg (Peters E347)

PROKOFIEV   Quintet, ob, cl, vln, vla, dbl bass, op. 39.
                    1927. 30 min. Adv. + / Tema. Andante
                    energico. Allegro sostenuto, ma con brio.
                    Adagio pesante. Allegro precipitato, ma
                    non presto. Andantino.

An excellent piece, but not an easy one to sight-read;
it requires much individual practice as well as ensemble rehearsal; the composer's harmonies create uncommon fingering
patterns.   The first movement is a set of variations on a
rather exotic theme; the second movement develops a theme
in contrapuntal style; the third, written in a meter of five
appears more complicated than it is--players should use the
simplified version which the publisher supplies and which
breaks down the five into measures of two and three beats.
The fourth movement is long, with continuous sound from the
winds, testing their endurance.   The fifth movement will
challenge the skills of the double-bass player.
      Cobbett, vol. 3, 138
Parts: Boosey; International; Kalmus
Score: International

CASELLA   Serenata, cl, bsn, tpt, vln, vc. 1927. 26
                  min. Adv. / Marcia. Minuetto. Not-
                  turno. Gavotte-Musette. Cavatina. Finale.

     In this ingratiating six-movement work each instrument
plays an active role, including the trumpet, whose part is
well integrated into the total sound fabric. Even the bassoon
and cello parts, which generally function as one, are independent of each other. The Gavotte is for winds alone and the
Cavatina for strings. Cobbett tells us that the Philadelphia
jury which awarded the Serenata a prize called it "an authentic model of purely Italian style in form and spirit and in
its characteristically continuous melodic flow...." The bassoon part is often in tenor clef; clarinet in B flat and A.
     Cobbett, vol. 3, 54-55
Parts: Universal Edition 8823
Score: Universal Edition Ph177

6 SEXTETS

*BRAHMS   Sextet, 2 vlns, 2 vlas, 2 vcs, no. 1, op.
18, B flat major. Pub. 1862. 40 min.
Adv. / Allegro ma non troppo. (Tema
con variazione) Andante ma moderato.
(Scherzo) Allegro molto. (Rondo) Poco
allegretto e grazioso.

The sextets op. 18 and op. 36 make good introductions
to Brahms. Op. 18 is easier to grasp, perhaps because of
its ingratiating first movement, whose themes are waltz-like.
No less attractive is the second movement, which opens with
a theme in the viola reminiscent of folk music and with an
accompaniment that sounds like a cembalon. When the cellists take their turn at embellishing the theme in this theme-
and-variations movement, the result may be marvelously
dramatic or disastrous, depending on how well the two cellists can play sweeping scale passages in unison! Toward
the end of the movement there is a tranquil mood set by a
shift to the major key; the movement closes with a return
to the theme in minor. In the Rondo Brahms often pairs
the lower instruments against the upper ones to create contrasts and question-answer effects. The movement is straightforward with a jovial close led by the solo viola. Brahms,
a violist, often freed viola parts from accompanimental roles
for soloistic ones.

    Cobbett, vol. 1, 163   Ferguson, 212-15
    Colles, 15-16   Keys, 22-24
    Drinker, 52-54   Mason, Brahms, 13-21
    Evans, vol. 1, 74-95
Parts: International; Peters 3906A
Score: Eulenberg (Peters E235); Lea 170 (with op. 36);
    Peters (Brahms Chamber Music for Strings, vol. 1)

*BRAHMS   Sextet, 2 vlns, 2 vlas, 2 vcs, no. 2, op.
36, G major. Pub. 1866. 40 min. Adv.
/ Allegro non troppo. (Scherzo) Allegro
non troppo. Poco adagio. Poco allegro.

Opus 36 contrasts with op. 18 in its overall texture and complexity; there is less tunefulness and more intricate counterpoint. The first movement has a notable pedal point which begins in the viola part. Reversing the usual order, Brahms puts the first movement in a triple meter and the Scherzo in duple. The Scherzo, a fughetto, takes on a stately quality; however, its Trio section comes as an abrupt contrast with an abandoned dance in 3/4 meter and in the contrasting major mode. As is the case with many Brahms Adagio movements, this one is lengthy and quite complex with a great deal of independence in the parts.

Cobbett, vol. 1, 170- 71
Colles, 25-27
Drinker, 63-67
Evans, vol. 1, 159-78

Ferguson, 215-18
Keys, 24-26
Mason, Brahms, 55-63
Tovey, Chamber Music, 245-46

Parts: International; Peters 3906B
Score: Eulenberg (Peters E236); Lea 170 (with op. 18); Peters (Brahms Chamber Music, vol. 1)

DVOŘÁK   Sextet, 2 vlns, 2 vlas, 2 vcs, op. 48 (B. 80), A major. 1818. 32 min. Int.-Adv. / Allegro moderato. (Dumka) Poco allegretto. (Furiant) Presto. (Finale) Tema con variazioni, allegretto grazioso, quasi andantino.

The ideal companion piece to the Brahms sextets; not too difficult to play, lyrical, sunny, and full of Slavic themes. The first movement, based on the folk ballad or dumka, is characterized by abrupt shifts in key, meter, and mood.

Cobbett, vol. 1, 357- 58

Sourek, 22-27

Parts: Artia; International; Simrock
Score: Artia; Eulenberg (Peters E337)

SCHOENBERG   Verklärte Nacht (Transfigured Night), 2 vlns, 2 vlas, 2 vcs, op. 4. 1889. 30 min. Adv.

This is more often heard in the composer's arrangement for string orchestra. He made two versions, one in 1917 and the other in 1943. Not far removed from the romantic idiom with its chromaticism and "floating" harmonies, it makes a good introduction to Schoenberg and 20th-century music for those "traditionalists." It is a music-drama in one movement, shaped to the five stanzas of Richard Dehmel's poem on which it is based. The players receive little rest;

there are frequent chromatic runs, tremolo passages, and
sixteenth-note figures.

Cobbett, vol. 2, 344   Robertson, 390-96
Cohn, Europe, 268   Whittall, 9-11
Parts: International; Universal Edition 366
Score: International; Universal Edition 3662

POULENC   Sextuor, pf, fl, ob, cl, hn, bsn. 1932-39.
                 20 min. Adv. / Allegro vivace. Très
                 vite et emporté. (Divertissement) Andantino.
                 (Finale) Prestissimo.

Most woodwind players are familiar with this effer-
vescent work, characteristic of Poulenc's élan. The first
movement opens energetically, comes to a halt suddenly, and
moves into a languorous theme by way of a bassoon cadenza.
The second movement opens in the style of Mozart and closes
in the style of Chopin, demonstrating Poulenc's eclecticism.
The Finale has tremendous rhythmic vitality and all the
"flash" the unsophisticated players relish.

Cohn, Europe, 239
Parts: Hansen
Score: Hansen

PROKOFIEV   Overture on Hebrew Themes, pf, cl, 2 vlns,
                 vla, vc, op. 34. Pub. 1922. 14 min. Int.

Great listener appeal, with its sinuous, repetitious
melody introduced by the clarinet; the piano and clarinet give
a unique tonal color to the ensemble. No obvious technical
problems; some aspects of the parts may create tedium for
the players, e.g., the strings have sustained passages of
tremolo and the piano part consists largely of repeated sixteenth-note passages in the right hand against accompanying
eighth notes in the left.

Cobbett, vol. 3, 137-38
Parts: Boosey; International; Kalmus
Score: International

BEETHOVEN   Sextet, 2 cls, 2 hns, 2 bsns, op. 71, E flat
                 major. 1796. 20 min. Int. / Adagio-
                 Allegro. Adagio. (Menuetto) Quasi allegret-
                 to. (Rondo) Allegro.

Classical in design in a fortuitous key for wind players
with euphonious and agreeable parts. After the Adagio curtain raiser the first movement is based primarily on a short

motif presented by the clarinet; the second movement is a
simple song which lends itself to melodic elaboration; the
Menuetto recalls the hunting horn and contains a charming
fugal Trio; the Rondo gives everyone a good workout on a
buoyant dotted rhythm theme.

Robertson, 304-5   Scherman, 203
Parts: Breitkopf; International; Musica Rara
Score: International

JANÁČEK   Mládí (Youth) Suite, fl, ob, cl, bass cl, hn,
                 bsn. 1926. 16 min. Adv. / Allegro.
                 Andante sostenuto. Vivace. Allegro anima-
                 to.

     Written when Janáček was 72, it conveys the antics as
well as the dreamy melancholy of his youth. Highly original,
devoid of clichés and remarkably contemporary in sound;
harmonies and rhythms evoke a Slavonic flavor. The addition of bass clarinet creates a much richer timbre than that
of the standard woodwind quintet. The bass clarinet part
(written in bass clef) is a grateful one; flute doubles on piccolo in the Vivace. Odd rhythmic groupings necessitate
working out the parts in a mechanical manner, but ultimately,
the players must free themselves of a mechanical approach
and capture the improvisatory quality of the music.
     Cohn, Europe, 149-50
Parts: Associated Music Publishers; Boosey
Score: Associated Music Publishers; Boosey

MOZART   Ein musikalischer Spass (A Musical Joke),
                 2 hns, 2 vlns, vla, vc, K. 522, F major.
                 1787. 22 min. Adv. / Allegro. (Min-
                 uetto) Maestoso. Adagio cantabile. Presto.

     In speaking of K. 522, Alfred Einstein suggests that
it is the negative key to Mozart's whole aesthetics. Mozart's
mockery consists, in part, of dissonances, trills and rhythmic
figures that last too long, awkward modulations, inappropriately
placed Alberti bass patterns, and a pointless violin cadenza.
The parody is subtle in some places, quite obvious in others
--an audience of musicians will chuckle all the way through.
     Ferguson, 73-74
Parts: International; Kalmus; Peters R2; Southern Music
        (Texas)
Score: Eulenberg (Peters E217); International

BEETHOVEN   Sextet, 2 hns, 2 vlns, vla, vc, op. 81b, E

flat major. 1794-95. 12 min. Adv. /
Allegro con brio. Adagio. Rondo.

Horn parts are virtuosic; string parts rudimentary
and in a low tessitura. The solo violin carries more of the
thematic material either as partner to one of the horns or
to provide relief for the horns. The horn parts are nicely
balanced between concerted passages (usually in thirds), imitative passages, antiphonal phrases, and periods of rest.
The first movement has a rudimentary development section,
in the minor mode.
Scherman, 203-4
Parts: International; Peters L192
Score: Lea 154 (with op. 20, op. 29, op. 137)

MOZART   Divertimenti, 2 obs, 2 hns, 2 bsns, no. 12,
                       K. 252, E flat major; no. 13, K. 253, F
                       major. 1776. 9 to 11 min. each. Adv.

Mozart wrote six divertimenti for this combination,
the others being K. 213, K. 240, K. 270, and K. 289. They
are suites with three to seven movements. Mozart's genius
for contrapuntal writing is evident even in this early incidental music. The first oboe and the horn parts are soloistic
in K. 252; K. 253's first movement is a beautifully elaborated
theme and variations.
Cobbett, vol. 2, 179
Parts: Breitkopf; Kalmus
Score: Breitkopf (K. 252); Eulenberg 35 (K. 253)

MENDELSSOHN   Sextet, pf, vln, 2 vlas, vc, dbl bass, op.
                       110, D major. 1824. 30 min. Int. -
                       Adv. / Allegro vivace. Adagio. (Min-
                       uetto) Agitato. Allegro vivace.

An early, lightweight piece with a virtuosic piano part
and unobtrusive string parts; outer movements are long, inner
ones brief. The last movement is considered more musically
significant than the others. Library purchase of this work
and other works of unusual instrumentation is advantageous
to patrons who would hesitate to purchase works that they
would play infrequently because of the difficulty in assembling
diverse instrumentations.
Horton, 17-18   Radcliffe, <u>Mendelssohn</u>,
                                        89-102
Parts: Litolff (Peters L636)

7 SEPTETS

*BEETHOVEN   Septet, cl, hn, bsn, vln, vla, vc, dbl bass, op. 20, E flat major. 1799-1800. Ded. Kaiserin Maria Theresia. 45 min. Adv. / Adagio-Allegro con brio. Adagio cantabile. Tempo di menuetto. Tema con variazioni. (Scherzo) Allegro molto e vivace. Andante con moto alla marcia-Presto.

The seven movements make this a divertimento. The highlights are the first, structured as a sonata-allegro form, and the fourth, a theme and variations. The second movement, Adagio, is also particularly beautiful, with the clarinet and the violin in the forefront. The entire work is a challenge to the violinist with many exposed passages and a cadenza in the final movement. The septet was accepted with great enthusiasm in Beethoven's time and its popularity persists. Beethoven was supposed to have been disdainful of the popularity of what he considered a lesser work of his youth.

Ferguson, 133   Scherman, 199-202
Robertson, 305-6
Parts: Breitkopf; International; Peters 2446
Score: Boosey; Eulenberg (Peters E12); Universal Edition Ph371

BERWALD   Septet, cl, hn, bsn, vln, vla, vc, dbl bass, "Stor" ("Grand"). 1828. 35 min. Adv. / (Introduzione) Adagio-Allegro molto. Poco adagio-Prestissimo-Adagio. (Finale) Allegro con spirito.

A sort of Swedish Charles Ives, Berwald is now receiving overdue recognition for his modest but unique contributions to the chamber music repertoire. A discussion of his work can be found in Franz Berwald by Robert Layton (London: Anthony Blond, 1959). The septet, an early work modeled on Beethoven's for the same instrumentation, is

128

discussed on pages 49 and 52.   Berwald's enfolding the Scherzo movement in the Adagio is unique.   The style is transparent, homophonic, and with a classical melodic approach.
Cobbett, vol. 1, 125
Parts: Edition Suecia/Stockholm Föreningen Svenske Tonsättare
Score: Edition Suecia/Stockholm Föreningen Svenske Tonsättare.

RAVEL   Introduction and Allegro, harp, fl, cl, 2
                vlns, vla, vc. 1905. Comm. Micheline
                Kahn. 15 min. Adv. / Très lent-Moins
                lent-Allegro.

Orchestral in concept, this miniature harp concerto is a marvelous demonstration of the sonorous and technical capabilities of the instrument.   Basically homophonic with three alternating themes and frequent changes of textural color; harp cadenzas separate the sections.   After a langorous introduction, momentum builds gradually to an Allegro in which the harp announces the main theme.   The close is brilliant. Some double tonguing for the winds; clarinet in A.
      Cobbett, vol. 2, 271   Stuckenschmidt, 80-81
Parts: Durand
Score: Durand

HINDEMITH   Septet, fl, ob, cl, bass cl, bsn, hn, tpt.
                1948. 18 min. Adv. / Lebhaft. (Inter-
                mezzo) Sehr langsam, frei. (Variationen)
                Mässig schnell. (Intermezzo) Sehr langsam.
                (Fuge alter Berner Marsch) Schnell.

A compact, straightforward work largely in contrapuntal style.   The last movement is an intricate fugue; the Intermezzi are very thin in texture; the middle movement is the highlight, with variations on a simple march theme.
      Cobbett, vol. 3, 15
Parts: Schott 919
Score: Schott 3540

SAINT-SAËNS   Septet, pf, tpt, 2 vlns, vla, vc, dbl bass,
                op. 65, E flat major. 1881. 17 min. Adv.
                / Préambule. Menuet. Intermède. Gavotte
                et Final.

Cobbett informs us that this suite was written for the French performing society, La Trompette, founded in 1860.

Textures are thin, with judicious treatment of piano and trumpet; a regimental call of the French army is incorporated into the final movement.   Trumpet in E flat.
          Cobbett, vol. 2, 324
Parts: Durand; International
Score: Durand; International

D'INDY   Suite in Olden Style, 2 fls, tpt, 2 vlns, vla,
                          vc/dbl bass, op. 24, D major.   1886.   22
                          min.   Int.-Adv.   /   Prélude.   Entrée.
                          Sarabande.   Menuet.   Rondo Française.

          A rather inane piece, but not without some charm; it warrants inclusion here as a companion piece to the slightly more substantial Saint-Saëns septet for trumpet, piano, and strings.   The trumpet part is fairly inactive until the last two movements.
Parts: Hamelle; International
Score: Hamelle; International

8 OCTETS

*MENDELSSOHN   Octet, 4 vlns, 2 vlas, 2 vcs, op. 20,
                E flat major.   Pub. 1832.   31 min.   Adv.
                /   Allegro moderato ma con fuoco.   An-
                dante.   Allegro leggierissimo.   Presto.

Mendelssohn was 16 when he composed this incredible
work, which swirls along, inspired by the realm of Oberon
and Titania.   This Scherzo movement preceded the famous
Scherzo from Midsummer Night's Dream.   String players
revel in the use of many of their resources, from heavy orchestral
effects to shimmering, transparent ones.   Humor abounds--
in the last movement the theme from Handel's Messiah,
"And He Shall Reign," is heard bouncing around.
        Cobbett, vol. 2, 129   Horton, 22-27
        Ferguson, 161-62   Robertson, 175-80
Parts: International; Peters 1782
Score: Eulenberg (Peters E59); International

*SCHUBERT   Octet, cl, hn, bsn, 2 vlns, vla, vc, dbl
                bass, op. posth. 166 (D. 803).   Pub. 1853.
                Ded. Graf Ferdinand Troyer.   50 min.
                Adv. / Adagio-Allegro.   Adagio.   (Scherzo)
                Allegro vivace.   Andante.   (Menuetto) Al-
                legretto.   Andante molto-Allegro.

For an evening of chamber music, a perfect companion
to the Beethoven Septet op. 20 which Schubert modeled on the
Beethoven work, adding a second violin for a more orchestral
texture.   Divertimento-like, with its several movements, it
challenges the players' endurance, especially the clarinet and
violin, which carry a great deal of the thematic material.
The other parts are not dull by any means--Schubert provides
a variety of textures and harmonic changes, especially in the
fourth movement which is a lengthy theme and variations.
The first and the last movement each begin with a mysterious,
foreboding introduction leading into a sprightly theme, but only

in the last movement does this solemn material return, near
the end.

Brent-Smith, 30-55   Robertson, 152-58
Einstein, Schubert,   Westrup, 13-18
   256-57
Ferguson, 153-55
Parts: Breitkopf; International; Peters 1849
Score: Eulenberg (Peters E60); Ricordi Pr472

MOZART   Serenade, 2 obs, 2 cls, 2 hns, 2 bsns, K.
                384a (388), C minor. 1782. 22 min. Adv.
                / Allegro. Andante. Menuetto in canone.
                Allegro.

Of the three wind serenades that Mozart wrote, this,
the last, is the most compact and terse. The others are
K. 361 and K. 375. Its key of C minor is unusual for serenade music, and its general mood and musical content far
more intimate than the customary outdoor music; it is difficult to think of it as incidental music; there is an unbelievable
variety of ideas. All the instruments share in solo ventures.
The third movement, a minuet in canon, is quite outstanding.
Einstein, Mozart,   Landon, 66-89
   205-6
Parts: Breitkopf; Broude
Score: Eulenberg; Kalmus (with 2 Divertimenti and 3 Serenades)

BEETHOVEN   Octet, 2 obs, 2 cls, 2 hns, 2 bsns, op.
                   103, E flat major. 1792. 22 min. Adv.
                   / Allegro. Andante. Menuetto. (Finale)
                   Presto.

Few concert-goers are aware of how marvelously rich
the sound of eight wind instruments can be and how stirring
the effect. This work bubbles over with good cheer; the
final movement is a real tour-de-force of wind virtuosity,
with the horns in the forefront.
Scherman, 39-40
Parts: Breitkopf; Broude; Musica Rara
Score: no information available

HAYDN   Octet, 2 obs, 2 cls, 2 hns, 2 bsns, Hob. II:
               F7, F major. 19 min. Int. / Allegro
               moderato. Andante con variazioni. (Menuet-
               to) Allegretto. (Finale) Allegro.

A harmonically simple and compact work, with Haydn's

playfulness evident throughout.   The second movement, in
which each instrument takes a turn at the elaboration of the
theme is a delight.   Haydn wrote many of these compositions
for either large wind groups or large string groups--the
former are called field-partitas, the latter, divertimenti.
In the strict sense, this is not chamber music, but outdoor
music.
Parts: International
Score: International

STRAVINSKY   Octet, fl, cl, 2 bsns, 2 tpts, 2 trbs.
                  1952. 16 min. Adv. / Sinfonia. Tema
                  con variazioni. Finale.

This work could serve as a primer to French and
American 20th-century music, so dominating an influence was
Stravinsky.   The pandiatonic textures found here became an
American trademark for decades.   The composer builds mass-
es of sound with little expressive intent; dynamics are de-
pendent, not on individual players, but on the number of instruments used in each passage and on the varying timbres;
dry effects call for much staccato playing; many strong accents and odd divisions of the beat.   The score, which is a
revision of the original 1923 score, calls for clarinet in A,
trumpet in C, trumpet in A, tenor trombone, and bass trombone.
      Cobbett, vol. 2, 466-67
Parts: Boosey
Score: Boosey

HINDEMITH   Octet, cl, bsn, hn, vln, 2 vlas, vc, dbl
                  bass. 1957-58. 26 min. Adv. / Breit.
                  (Varienten) Mässig bewegt. Langsam. Sehr
                  lebhaft. (Fuge und drei altmodische Tänze)
                  Walzer, Polka, Galopp.

The outer movements are active with much interplay
of parts; the inner movements are more sustained.   This
would be a good companion piece to the Schubert Octet for
an evening of chamber music--it would be helpful to have a
second violinist who could play viola on the Hindemith.
      Cobbett, vol. 3, 15-16   Cohn, Europe, 115
Parts: Schott 4686
Score: Schott 4595

BEETHOVEN   Rondino, 2 obs, 2 cls, 2 hns, 2 bsns, op.
                  posth. WoO 25, E flat major. Pub. 1829.
                  8 min. Adv. / Andante.

This all-too-brief gem contains some beautiful melodic elaborations in which all the instruments share--the horns are allowed a little more prominence than usual.
Parts: Breitkopf
Score: Breitkopf

VARÈSE   Octandre, fl, cl, ob, bsn, hn, tpt, trb, dbl
                         bass. 1924. Ded. E. Robert Schmitz. 7
                         min. Adv. + / Assez lent. Très vif et
                         nerveux. Grave.

A living-room rehearsal is to be avoided, unless one has tolerant neighbors. Varèse writes clusters of sound with intervals that are close and dissonant and makes demands on volume of sound; there are some savage passages. Varèse creates marvelous effects with these clusters of sounds--he does not use chords in the traditional harmonic sense or pitches in the traditional melodic sense. Additional effects are created through string harmonics, glissandi, flutter tonguing, rapid crescendi and diminuendi. Rhythms are difficult; odd placements of notes for punctuated effects; rhythmic figures on one pitch are frequent. The trumpet and oboe parts are soloistic; flute doubles piccolo; clarinet doubles E flat sopranino. Trumpet in C; tenor trombone.
       Cobbett, vol. 3, 165   Ouellette, 80-81
       Cohn, Europe, 215
Parts: Ricordi
Score: Ricordi

LAZAROF   Octet, fl, ob, cl, bass cl, bsn, tpt, hn, trb.
                         1967. 10 min. Adv. + / Variation I.
                         Variation II.

This may sound ultra modern to some ears; however, the players are not required to produce any unconventional sounds. Lazarof utilized conventional techniques to achieve his artistic purpose. In the course of the four or five minutes required for the first movement, 11 variations are heard. Pauses between variations become increasingly shorter, from five seconds down to one second, and the tempo increases with each variation. Instruments are grouped by timbre-- flute/oboe/clarinet in one, bass clarinet/bassoon in another, and trumpet/horn/trombone in the third. The second movement variations are treated more linearly and there are no pauses separating them. Instruments are grouped thus: flute/ oboe/clarinet/trumpet against horn/bassoon/bass clarinet/ trombone. Parts are angular; intervals close and dissonant;

rapid dynamics changes and counting difficulties.   A conductor
would be in order.   Parts available on a rental basis from
publisher.
Parts: Associated Music Publishers
Score: Associated Music Publishers

MOZART   Serenade, 2 obs, 2 cls, 2 basset hns, 4
            hns, 2 bsns, dbl bass/contrabsn, no. 10,
            K. 370a (361), B flat major, "Gran Partita."
            1781. 42 min. Adv. / Largo-Allegro
            molto. Menuetto. Adagio. (Menuetto)
            Allegretto. (Romanza) Adagio. (Thema mit
            Variationen) Andante. (Rondo) Allegro molto.

    Most of the serenades written during Mozart's time
were written as incidental music, more often than not commissioned for festive occasions. This delightful serenade is
typical of the outdoor spirit of those compositions, but Mozart's exploitation of instrumental color is far ahead of the
time. Among the many magical moments is the Adagio in
which the clarinet and oboe spin a lovely melody above an
ostinato rhythm in the lower winds. Usually played with
contrabassoon; however, Mozart is supposed to have specified
double bass. Alto clarinets are usually substituted for basset
horns. A luxury purchase which would give wind players
access to wind music few can afford to buy.
    Landon, 66-89
Parts: Breitkopf; Musica Rara; Peters; Rubank
Score: Eulenberg; Kalmus (with 2 Divertimenti and 3 Sere-
    nades)

DVOŘÁK   Serenade, 2 obs, 2 cls, 3 hns, 2 bsns, con-
            trabsn, vc, dbl bass, op. 44 (B. 77), D
            minor. 1878. Ded. Louis Ehlert. 25 min.
            Adv. / Moderato quasi marcia. (Menuetto)
            Tempo de menuetto. Andante con moto.
            (Finale) Allegro molto.

    This engaging work is a real treat for the wind players,
particularly oboes and clarinets, allowing them to assume
soloistic roles generally taken by strings in an orchestra setting. It opens with a stirring village march which will re-

appear near the end of the Finale. The Menuetto and Finale
are based on folk dances; the Andante, by contrast, is a
fervent song. Clarinets in A; however, a part for B flat is
furnished by some publishers. A conductor is necessary for
a public performance.
Parts: International; Kalmus
Score: International

STRAUSS   Serenade, 2 fls, 2 obs, 2 cls, 4 hns, 2
                     bsns, contrabsn, op. 7. 1882. 12 min.
                     Adv.

    A large wind group has a rich and unique sound; in
this case Strauss' rich Wagnerian harmonies make it especially lush. The flutes add brilliance to the darker sound of the
lower winds. Composed when Strauss was in his teens, the
work relies on classical structure. In one movement with
a principal melody appearing after a long, 30-measure introduction. A counter-melody appears along with a reiterative
triplet pattern which becomes a predominating figure as the
piece progresses. The meter indicates two beats per mea-
sure; however, it is usually felt in four. The contrabassoon
part may be played by tuba.
Parts: International; Southern Music (Texas); Universal Edi-
     tion
Score: International

PISTON   Divertimento for Nine Instruments, fl, ob,
                     cl, bsn, 2 vlns, vla, vc, dbl bass, op. 1.
                     1946. 12 min. Adv. / Allegro. Tran-
                     quillo. Vivo.

    In the two sprightly outer movements Piston employs
short motivic fragments in a lean, non-gratuitous style with
plenty of staccato, pizzicato, syncopation, and meter shifts.
The syncopation seems more Gallic in identity than American.
The middle movement is contemplative, with a very effective
reduced instrumentation. The overall effect is an orchestral
one.
     Cobbett, vol. 3, 160
Parts: Associated Music Publishers
Score: Associated Music Publishers (included with parts)

BRITTEN   Sinfonietta, fl, cl, ob, hn, bsn, 2 vlns, vla,
                     vc, dbl bass, op. 1. 1932. Ded. Frank
                     Bridge. 25 min. Adv. / Poco presto ed
                     agitato. (Variations) Andante lento. (Taran-
                     tella) Presto vivace.

A well-organized work of recurring motifs which are set out in a mosaic, fragmentary manner during the brief first movement. The middle movement begins with the winds playing fragments which dovetail--the tones seem to melt one into the other. Towards the end of the movement the viola begins a perpetual-motion figure which leads into the last movement. The Tarantella contains a slow interlude in which the bassoon solos against harmonics in the double bass; the clarinet leads the way out of the interlude with a rapid, tongued perpetual-motion figure.

Cobbett, vol. 3, 90-91
Parts: Boosey
Score: Boosey

SCHUBERT   Der Hirt auf dem Felsen (The Shepherd on
                  the Rock), pf, voice, cl, op. posth. 129
                  (D. 965). Pub. 1830. For Anna Milder-
                  Hauptmann. 12 min. Adv. / Andantino-
                  Allegretto.

   The text tells of the shepherd's longing for his love as
he scans the horizon and hears his echo. The clarinet introduces the melody with the piano providing a triplet accompaniment figure which continues throughout the first section
of the song. When the voice enters, there is dialogue between voice and clarinet, imitating the echo. When the shepherd thinks of the winter ahead, the mood of the piece becomes desolate--the song turns to the minor mode and the
accompaniment slips into a duple pattern. Then there is a
transition by way of a quasi-cadenza for clarinet, imitating
the shepherd's flute. The last section reflects the joy the
shepherd feels in thinking of the coming of spring--the song
becomes ebullient and ends with a bravura passage for clarinet. Flute or violin may substitute for clarinet. Alternate
parts are usually provided by publisher. Voice part is high,
usually sung by a soprano.
   Einstein, Schubert, 302-
  3
Parts: Augener; Breitkopf; Schirmer

SCHUBERT   Auf dem Strom (On the River), pf, voice,
                  hn, op. posth. 119 (D. 943). Pub. 1829.
                  For Joseph Rudolf Lewy. 12 min. Adv. /
                  Mässig.

   The song is a melancholic farewell of a lover who is
being carried out to sea on the river's current. Schubert's
harmonies are in perfect accord with the shifting nuances of
the poem. The timbre of the horn is well suited to the mood.
As in the song above, the piano plays a subdued role to the
dialogue of voice (usually tenor) and horn.

Einstein, Schubert, 302-3
Parts: Augener; Breitkopf; Schirmer
Score: Kalmus 1092

BARBER   Dover Beach, medium voice, string quartet,
                  op. 3. 1931. 10 min. Adv.

    Samuel Barber was a gifted vocalist as well as com-
poser, and he sang the first performance of this work, a
setting of the Matthew Arnold poem. The voice part remains
within the range of an octave; there are no large or unusual
intervals; the string parts are fairly subdued and present no
difficulties.
Parts: Schirmer
Score: Schirmer 15

VAUGHAN WILLIAMS On Wenlock Edge (from A Shropshire
                  Lad by A. E. Housman), pf, voice, string
                  quartet. 1909. 22 min. Adv.

    This very moving song cycle for tenor voice includes
"On Wenlock Edge," "From Far, from Eve and Morning,"
"Is My Team Ploughing," "Oh, When I Was in Love with
You," "Bredon Hill," and "Clun." "Bredon Hill" is a particularly moving poem about two lovers in which the composer
admirably captures the drama. The string quartet is not es-
sential--the piano part contains cues in its absence, but its
absence diminishes the total effect. It makes interpretative
rather than technical demands. The composer's other song
cycles which would make nice additions to the collection are
Ten Blake Songs for voice and oboe (Boosey & Hawkes) and
Eight Housman Songs for voice and violin (Oxford University
Press).
        Cobbett, vol. 2, 584-   Cohn, Europe, 314
          86
Parts: Boosey
Score: Boosey

RAVEL   Trois Poèmes de Mallarmé, pf, 2 fls,
                  2 cls, voice, string quartet.   1913.
                  12 min. Adv. + / Soupir. Placet futile.
                  Surgi de la croupe et du bond.

    Representative of Ravel's excursion into Schoenberg's
atonal world. The pointillistic technique makes it a difficult
work to assemble and requires an expert soprano; a conductor
is recommended. The changes of mood and the poetic effects

are exquisitely brought forth in Ravel's iridescent writing.
An edition for voice and piano is available.   One flute doubles
piccolo, one clarinet doubles bass clarinet.
    Cobbett, vol. 2, 275   Myers, 135-42
    Demuth, 135-43   Stuckenschmidt, 130-32
Parts: Durand

DALLAPICCOLA   Goethe-Lieder, 3 cls, voice. 1953.   9
              min.   Adv. +

      There is a great deal of intensity and drama in these
seven songs for B flat clarinet, E flat clarinet, bass clarinet, and mezzo-soprano.   Dynamics and accents are precisely
indicated; however, the extreme independence of the parts
makes the ensemble complex.   In some of the movements the
composer uses just one or two of the clarinets with the voice.
The analysis which follows is offered by musicologist Robert
Zieff (there is also a discussion of the songs by Hans Nathan
in Musical Quarterly, July 1958, pages 289-310).
    "Textures which grew out of the 20th-century Viennese
school are exemplified in the first of these songs by the
pairing of instruments in 9ths, then in 7ths, followed by
motivic interplay based on a germ (a minor second followed by a major second in inversion and/or retrograde)
suggested in the vocal line.   The germ, now made into
leaps of the seventh, opens the second song, a canon for
voice and E flat clarinet.   The same tone row as in the
second song, in conjunct intervals, opens the third song,
but with its second half transposed, this time forming a
three-part canon, the B flat clarinet line in augmentation
(without the second half transposed) and the E flat clarinet in inversion.   The composer stresses the unity of
these movements by directing that there be only a short
pause between them.   The germ, as descending leaps in
quasi-stretto for the clarinets, introduces, closes, and
even turns up in the course of the fourth song.   This
song reshapes the original tone row of the first song--
the voice this time follows a two-clarinet canon based
on the row in longer values which later becomes a three-
clarinet canon in short values.   As song four was to one,
five opens with the tone row of two--the voice and E flat
clarinet in canon, but in inversion here and with the bass
clarinet added in augmentation.   And so, song six begins
with the germ moving conjunctly as in three, but the
bass clarinet replaces the other clarinets which were
present in song three.   The germs dominate both parts
throughout this song.   A quasi-stretto of the germ (con-

junct stepwise) opens song seven suggested by a similar usage in song four (as would be expected!). But this time the voice joins in augmentation, continuing with the row. Alas, the stretto (as in song four) turns up. The tone row of song one in canon at a distance of an eighth is in the B flat clarinet and voice and ends with a texture similar to that at the end of song one. "

Cobbett, vol. 3, 58-59   Cohn, Europe, 72, 75
Parts: Suvini Zerboni
Score: Suvini Zerboni

ANNOTATED BIBLIOGRAPHY

Abraham, Gerald. Beethoven's Second-Period Quartets.
(The Musical Pilgrim.) London: Oxford University Press,
1942. This slender volume covers opus 59 through opus
95; brief analyses geared to the amateur musician and
music lover.

Adorno, Theodor W. Introduction to the Sociology of Music,
translated by E. B. Ashton. New York: Seabury Press,
1976. A series of lectures delivered in 1961-62 at
Frankfort University which the author refers to as "spontaneous reflection" with no effort to be systematic. In
the Foreword Adorno points out that sociologists have
chided "spontaneous reflection" as anything but sociolo-
gical. From another viewpoint, one music critic assured
him that the lectures contain nothing not already known
to every musician. Among the topics is "Chamber
Music," beginning on page 85. It is not easy reading--
although the main ideas can be readily comprehended,
Adorno's intricacies of thought are not easy to follow.

Alker, Hugo. Blockflöten-Bibliographie. Wilhelmshaven:
Heinrichshofen's Verlag, 1966. A list of the recorder
repertoire, methods, and literature; repertoire list divided by number and combination of instruments; entries
give composer/author, title, instrumentation, publisher,
and publisher number.

_____. Blockflöten-Bibliographie Nachtrag und Gesamtre-
gister. Wilhelmshaven: Heinrichshofen's Verlag, 1969.
Recorder repertoire supplement which contains the composer index to Blockflöten-Bibliographie by Alker, plus
a section on music for flute and guitar.

Altmann, Wilhelm. Kammermusik-Katalog. Leipzig: Friedrich Hofmeister, 1945. A classed listing of chamber
music combinations starting with ten instruments and
proceeding to two; sample groupings are wind with string,

chamber music with piano, harp combinations, guitar
combinations, etc.   Entry includes composer, title, opus
number, date of composition, and publisher; composer
index; list of publishers with their addresses; covers
period 1841-1944.   See also the Richter Kammermusik-
Katalog, below.

Auer, Leopold.   Violin Masterworks and Their Interpretation.
New York: Carl Fischer, 1925.   Rudimentary analyses
with interpretive comments; contains a valuable chapter
on outstanding works of the older Italian composers.

Bachmann, Alberto.   An Encyclopedia of the Violin, translated by Frederick H. Martens.   London: The Library
Press, 1925.   Includes analyses of some master violin
works such as Tartini's "Devil's Trill" sonata and Beethoven's "Kreutzer" sonata.

Barrett, Henry.   The Viola: Complete Guide for Teachers
and Students.   University: University of Alabama Press,
1972.   The first chapter, "Literature for Viola," in addition to original music, contains transcriptions, methods,
graded solos, and representative programs for advanced
players.   The appendix "Viola Music in Print" is divided
into five sections: study material; solo pieces; large
works; selected works with various instrumentations;
viola d'amore.   The section "Large Works" contains the
sonatas.   A publisher directory is included.

Barrett-Ayres, Reginald.   Joseph Haydn and the String Quartet.   New York: Schirmer, 1974.   Discussion proceeds
chronologically; helpful summaries of characteristics
with frequent diagrams; emphasis is on tonal structure;
many musical examples.   Discusses Mozart and Beethoven
quartets as they relate to Haydn's; extensive bibliography.

A Basic Music Library for Schools Offering Undergraduate
Degrees in Music.   Washington, D. C. : National Association of Schools of Music, 1967.   Suggestions for books,
periodicals, and study scores.   Section on books divides
into anthologies, dictionaries, bibliographies, etc. ; section on study scores divides by form and instrumentation;
publishers given.

Berkowitz, Freda Pastor.   Popular Titles and Subtitles of
Musical Compositions, 2d ed. Metuchen, N. J. : Scarecrow Press, 1975.   An annotated list by "popular" title
with foreign counterparts in brackets; composer index;

bibliography; interesting annotations; includes many obscure titles.

Braunstein, Joseph, ed.   Thematic Catalog of the Collected
Works of Brahms, enlarged ed. Ars Musica Press, 1956.
A fourth revision of the 1907 Simrock catalog; lists all
original works and original arrangements in chronological
order; includes a classed index, a title index, and a
first-line index for the vocal works.

Brent-Smith, Alexander.   Schubert Quartet in D minor and
Octet.   (The Musical Pilgrim, ed. by Dr. Arthur Somer-
vell.) London: Oxford University Press, 1927.   Move-
ment-by-movement analyses with musical examples; intended for the layman.

Bristol Public Libraries Catalogue of Music Scores.   Bristol,
England: City and County of Bristol Public Libraries,
1959.   Lists music which may be borrowed; one dictio-
nary sequence encompasses composer, instrument, and
form; the section on chamber music begins with trios and
ends with nonets; classification number and color code of
the library are indicated, plus opus number, key, instrumentation, availability of score and parts.

British Broadcasting Corporation Music Library.   Chamber
Music Catalogue.   London: The BBC, 1965.   Scope includes unaccompanied solos, solos for various instruments and piano, duets for various combinations; ends
with octets; basic division between groups with keyboard
and groups without; each citation gives opus number, key,
instrumentation, year of composition, editor/arranger,
BBC catalog number, duration (when available); composer
index.   Some of the other BBC catalogs are Choral and
Opera, Piano and Organ, and Song.

The British Catalogue of Music.   London: The British Library Bibliographic Services Division, 1957-.   Lists
musical literature as well as scores and parts; literature
appears also in the British National Bibliography.   Based
on material deposited at the Copyright Receipt Office of
the British Library.   It does not cumulate, necessitating
use of the annuals; there is composer, title, and subject
access; classification scheme by Eric Coates.   A sample
of the scheme: N-Chamber Music; NU-Wind, Strings and
Keyboard; NV-Winds and Strings; NX-Strings and Keyboard.   Full publishing information in the entries.

Brüchle, Bernhard. Horn Bibliographie. Wilhelmshaven:
    Heinrichshofen's Verlag, 1970. A good source of pub-
    lishers of any combination of instruments using horn.
    Contents include sections for horn solo, two horns, horn
    and piano, etc. plus sections for unusual couplings such
    as horn with guitar and horn with harp; goes to nine in-
    struments with a separate category for ten or more;
    composer index; black-and-white plates of horns from
    various periods.

Bryant, E. T. Music. New York: Philosophical Library,
    1965. The introduction states that this is a survey of
    some 250 books about music, mainly in print at the time
    of writing, and nearly all in English. The section on
    repertoire has many excellent suggestions; unfortunately,
    quite a few are not in print, including a particularly in-
    teresting book by Aulich and Heimeran, called The Well-
    Tempered String Quartet, translated and issued by Novel-
    lo in 1948.

_____. Music Librarianship: A Practical Guide. Lon-
    don: James Clark & Co. , 1959. Contains a useful ap-
    pendix on instrumental music, chamber music, piano
    solos, vocal solos, instrumental solos with keyboard ac-
    companiment, etc. Much of the music suggested is by
    lesser-known British composers; many items annotated,
    giving information on the works and their editions.

Burghauser, Jarmil. Antonín Dvořák Thematic Catalogue:
    Bibliography: Survey of Life and Work. Prague: Artia,
    1960. Table of Contents and Introduction in Czech, Ger-
    man, and English; a chronological survey that includes
    sketches, piano arrangements, and unfinished works; bib-
    liography includes periodical articles; indices by both
    form and by opus number; discography included.

Canadian Music Centre. Catalogue of Chamber Music Avail-
    able on Loan from the Library of the Canadian Music
    Centre. Toronto: the Centre, 1967. Supplement, 1971.
    Explanatory notes in English and French; a composer list
    which gives brief biographical information, address of
    composer, title, duration, dedication, dates of composi-
    tion and first performance, publisher of scores and parts,
    available tapes or records, degree of difficulty, and a
    brief annotation. Works listed by instrumentation also;
    appendix includes a history of Canadian music, a bib-
    liography, discography, list of publishers, and principal

music libraries. Many of the works are in manuscript; many of the recordings have been made by the Centre itself.

Carner, Mosco. Alban Berg: The Man and the Work. London: Gerald Duckworth, 1975. An attractive volume, with large, well-produced music examples; works grouped by form with an index of names and an index of musical examples.

Cobbett, Walter Willson, comp. and ed. Cobbett's Cyclopedic Survey of Chamber Music, 2d ed. with supplementary material edited by Colin Mason. 3 vols. London: Oxford University Press, 1963. Most articles are about composers with a few on subjects such as "American chamber music"; tables of composers' works precede articles; tables include dates of compositions, original publishers, opus numbers, keys, and instrumentations. Discussions vary in detail--the major works usually receive lengthy analyses; style varies with individual article writers. Volume three is a supplement for 20th-century music; extensive bibliography includes many periodical articles; much of the material is out of print. Cobbett may be dated in certain regards, and erroneous here and there, but it is still the most comprehensive source of information for chamber music and indispensable to practically any library music collection.

Cohn, Arthur. The Collector's Twentieth-Century Music in the Western Hemisphere. Philadelphia: Lippincott, 1961. Reprinted, New York: Da Capo, 1972. Discusses recorded music of 23 Americans, one Argentinian, one Brazilian, and two Mexicans; includes a capsule survey of the recordings up to May, 1960; brief entries arranged under each composer by form.

_____. Twentieth-Century Music in Western Europe; The Compositions and the Recordings. Philadelphia: Lippincott, 1965. There seems to be a good representation of nationalities in this counterpart to Cohn's book on music in the Western hemisphere; includes expatriates such as Schoenberg, Toch, and Hindemith.

Colles, H. C. The Chamber Music of Brahms. London: Oxford University Press, 1933. Originally written to accompany a series of performances; introductory notes on Brahms' life and the situations which surrounded his chamber music works; discusses the various versions of certain works.

Composers' Guild of Great Britain. Chamber Music by Living
    British Composers. British Music Information Center,
    1969. An arrangement by composer giving date of com-
    positions, instrumentation, duration, publisher, and avail-
    ability. Listings for three instruments or more.

Cooke, Deryck. "The Unity of Beethoven's Late Quartets,"
    Music Review 24 (1963): 30-49. Attempts to show "that
    the set of five constitutes a self-contained unity, a single
    continuous act of creation, in which Beethoven persistently
    developed certain implications of two basic pitch-patterns
    . . . . "

Coolidge, Richard A. "Form in the String Quartets of Franz
    Schubert," Music Review 32 (1971): 309-25. A case
    against the accusations of Schubert's formal inadequacies
    and/or deficiencies; author suggests that the quartets
    are not weak compared to Beethoven's, but differently
    conceived and differently projected.

Cowling, Elizabeth. The Cello. New York: Scribner's,
    1975. Discusses cello literature from early Baroque to
    20th century with a good view of the sonata literature;
    other chapters on cellists and instruments; black-and-
    white plates of some rare instruments.

Davies, J. H. Musicalia: Sources of Information in Music.
    Oxford: Pergamon Press, 1966. The author is Music
    Librarian of the BBC: chapter six is "The Chamber
    Musician and Instrumentalist"; mentions select lists which
    appear in sources such as Notes and Fontes Artis Musi-
    cae.

Decker, Richard G. , comp. A Bibliography of Music for
    Three Heterogeneous Brass Instruments Alone and in
    Chamber Ensembles. Oneonta, N. Y. : Swift-Dorr Pub-
    lications, 1976. Core of bibliography is detailed list by
    composer of published and unpublished works for brass
    trio; in chart form; includes title, length, level of dif-
    ficulty, ranges, use of mutes, publishers, cost, composi-
    tional techniques, and brief annotations. Enlightening
    introduction on growth of repertoire, outstanding works,
    and compositional techniques found most often in brass
    music.

Demuth, Norman. Ravel. (The Master Musician Series,
    edited by Eric Blom.) London: J. M. Dent, 1947.
    Claims to be the first biography in English on Ravel;

an example of how the passage of time can show opinion
about composers to be erroneous and prejudiced. Demuth, although apologetic at times, writes well about
the works. The first half of the book is a biographical
account of the works; the second section is arranged by
form. Chapter eleven is "Chamber Music." Includes
a catalog of works and a bibliography.

Deutsch, Otto Erich. Schubert; Thematic Catalogue of All
    His Works in Chronological Order. London: J. M.
    Dent, 1951. Complete information on the publication,
    literature, location of manuscripts, etc.; three indices--
    general, author, and classed; several appendices, some
    of which are for spurious works, unpublished works,
    and concordances.

Drinker, Henry S. The Chamber Music of Johannes Brahms.
    Philadelphia: Elkan, 1932. Originally prepared as pro-
    gram notes for the Brahms centenary celebration in
    Philadelphia, the arrangement is based on that program
    order; introductory biographical notes.

Dunhill, Thomas F. Chamber Music. London: Macmillan,
    1913. A treatise directed toward the student of composi-
    tion; chapter headings by form; spends some time discus-
    sing the meaning of chamber music and offers what he
    thinks would be a better term, namely, "Concerted Sonata
    Music."

_____. Mozart's String Quartets. 2 vols. (The Musical
    Pilgrim, edited by Dr. Arthur Somervell.) London: Ox-
    ford University Press, 1927. Reprinted, Westport,
    Conn.: Greenwood Press, 1970. A general approach
    with music examples; list of recordings available in 1927
    is interesting to compare with today's; a typical comment:
    "The Andante shows, perhaps for the first time in Mo-
    zart's chamber music, a real master of contrapuntal
    methods, and, incidentally, the use of mutes."

Eagon, Angelo. Catalog of Published Concert Music by
    American Composers, 2d ed. Metuchen, N. J.: Scare-
    crow Press, 1971. Two supplements, 1971, 1974. The
    criteria for inclusion are that the composer be native-
    born or naturalized before age 26 and that his contribu-
    tion be a significant one. Entries are grouped into the
    following categories: voice; instrumental solo; instrumen-
    tal ensemble; concert jazz; percussion; orchestra; opera;
    band. Each entry lists composer, title, date, instrumen-

tation, vocal ranges, type of accompaniment, duration,
publisher of score and/or parts, and rental information.
Indices for composers and authors and for sources of
texts.

Einstein, Alfred. Mozart: His Character, His Work, translated by Arthur Mendel and Nathan Broder. New York:
Oxford University Press, 1965. The author tells us in
his prefatory remarks that this is not an introduction to
Mozart's works, but rather it addresses itself to those
who already know and love his works. Einstein has
been successful in avoiding making this a mere catalog--
it is warmly written. The contents are divided into five
large sections: "The Man," "The Musician," "The Instrumental Works," "The Vocal Works," and "Opera." The
section on instrumental works is divided into chamber
music for strings, divertimento, cassation, chamber
music including clavier, etc. At the end there is a useful catalog of works arranged by Köchel number which
gives the page numbers where each work is mentioned.

_____. Schubert: A Musical Portrait. New York: Ox-
ford University Press, 1951. Contents arranged in a
chronological framework with 13 chapter headings, ranging from "Childhood and Youth" to "Illness and Death";
index of works divided into instrumental and vocal.

Evans, Edwin. Handbook to the Chamber Music of Johannes
Brahms. 2 vols. 1912. Reprinted, New York: Burt
Franklin, 1970. The author describes his work as an
"historical and descriptive account of each work with exhaustive structural, thematic and rhythmical analyses,
and a complete rhythmic chart of each movement." The
arrangement is by opus number with analyses and remarks
movement by movement. At the beginning of each entry
the person to whom it was dedicated is mentioned, as
well as other arrangements of the work made by the
composer; there is a unique index to music examples
wherein the movements are divided structurally and the
page numbers are given for each portion.

Ewen, David. Solo Instrumental and Chamber Music: Its
Story Told Through the Lives and Works of Its Foremost
Composers. (Mainstream of Music, vol. 3.) New York:
Franklin Watts, 1974. A survey type book, somewhat
superficial in manner; however, it fills a great need for
an elementary book on chamber music; it could be used

as a text book for a music appreciation class; the format
is most attractive, with many photographs; glossary of
terms; index.

Farish, Margaret K. String Music in Print. 2d ed. New York:
Bowker, 1973. This absolutely indispensable volume
first came out in 1965, its supplement in 1968. In addition to listing solo music for strings, the guide lists
music for diverse combinations, arranged by number of
instruments and subdivided by instrumentation. It includes a large section on trio sonatas and one on voice
with instruments. The list of scores is arranged by
composer; collections can be found by title or editor.
Publishing information includes available separates as
well as collections; editors' names are given in parentheses after publishers' names; a list of publishers' and
distributors' addresses is supplied.

Ferguson, Donald D. Image and Structure in Chamber Music.
Minneapolis: University of Minnesota Press, 1964. There
is more specific information about individual composers
and individual works than the title implies; while most
chapters stress one composer, a few center on topics
such as nationalistic chamber music or the beginnings
of chamber music. Each chapter begins with an overview and then discusses works from small to large, beginning with the sonata literature; music examples included; overall, a good selective reference source.

Fiske, Roger. Beethoven's Last Quartets. (The Musical
Pilgrim.) 1940. Reprinted, London: Oxford University
Press, 1944. Written in an easily understood style with
musical examples; introductory material on the style and
textural changes in Beethoven's output.

Frank, Alan. "The Chamber Music," in Grieg: A Symposium,
edited by Gerald Abraham. 1948. Norman: University
of Oklahoma Press, 1950. One of the few articles in
print on the subject; other topics in the book include the
piano music, song, and the orchestral music; chro-
nology and bibliography.

Gérard, Yves, comp. Thematic, Bibliographical and Critical
Catalog of the Works of Luigi Boccherini, Under the Aus-
pices of Germaine de Rothschild, translated by Andreas
Mayor. London: Oxford University Press, 1969. An
excellent guide through the maze of Boccherini's works;
three divisions--chamber, orchestra, and vocal; includes

a chronological table, bibliography, discography, and a
unique index of publishers which enumerates the works
in each publisher's catalog by the Gérard number.

Gillespie, James E., Jr. The Reed Trio: An Annotated
Bibliography of Original Published Works. (Detroit Studies in Music Bibliography, no. 20.) Detroit: Information Coordinators, 1971. Excellent annotations, summa-
rizing not only style but performance considerations; extensive notes on the author's methodology.

Gregory, Robin. The Horn: A Comprehensive Guide to the
Modern Instrument and Its Music. New York: Praeger,
1969. Chapter 25 is "The Horn in Chamber Music";
Appendix C, "A List of Music for the Horn," includes
sections for horn and piano, horn(s) with brass, arrangements for brass ensembles, chamber music, and horn
with voice.

_____. The Trombone: The Instrument and its Music.
New York: Praeger, 1973. The section "The Music"
is divided into: (1) trombone and piano; (2) trombone
and orchestra; (3) trombone(s) alone; (4) brass ensembles;
(5) chamber music; (6) trombone with voice. Section
"Sources" refers to some periodical articles on chamber
music for trombone; extensive list of publishers; complete
purchasing data.

Grodner, Murray. Comprehensive Catalog of Available Literature for the Double Bass, 3d ed. Bloomington, Ind.:
Lemur Musical Research, 1974. Extensive directions
for use, because so many items such as source and instrumentation are coded; large list of publishers; three
main sections--"Methods," "Etudes and Orchestra Studies,"
and "Solo Literature and Chamber Music." The section
on chamber music is divided into 18 parts, beginning
with two basses and going up to 14 instruments, plus
miscellaneous groupings; includes a discography.

Hadow, W. H. Beethoven's Op. 18 Quartets. (The Musical
Pilgrim.) London: Oxford University Press, 1948. Simple analyses geared to the layman.

Hayward, John D. Chamber Music for Amateurs: Notes
from a Library. (The Strad Library, no. 22.) New
York: Scribner's, 1923. This little book, which must
be a collector's item by now, was written by an amateur
player with comments directed toward other amateurs; it

is a delight to read, it is so charmingly written; some
of the works chosen are no longer popular; however, it
gives a good insight into what kind of material was most
appealing to amateurs at that time.

Heller, George N. Ensemble Music for Wind and Percussion
Instruments: A Catalog. Washington, D. C. : Music
Educators' National Conference, 1970. Includes much
easy material and many collections for either woodwind,
brass, or percussion ensembles, but no mixed ensembles
as the title might imply; five levels of difficulty and
graded according to range, key, rhythmic patterns, intervals, and tempo.

Helm, Sanford. Catalog of Chamber Music for Wind Instruments. Ann Arbor, Mich. : National Association of College Wind and Percussion Instrument Instructors, 1952.
Reprinted, New York: Da Capo Press, 1969. Lists
music for three to 12 players; no teaching material included; includes just a few transcriptions and/or arrangements.

Hill, Richard S. "Arnold Schoenberg: String Trio, op. 45,"
Notes 8 (1950): 127-29. A thorough analysis of the tone-
row structure of the trio.

Hoboken, Anthony von. Joseph Haydn: Thematisch-biblio-
graphisches Werkverzeichnis. 2 vols. Mainz: B.
Schott's Söhne, 1957. Groups the works into vocal and
instrumental; string quartets are found in section three
of instrumental music and piano trios in section 15; complete information on autographs, original editions, literature about, etc.

Horton, John. Mendelssohn Chamber Music. (BBC Music
Guides.) Seattle: University of Washington Press, 1972.
The BBC Music Guide series now includes over two dozen
books, several of them on chamber music; slim, and
usually not more than 60 pages long, they contain good
analyses linked with brief biographical material; Horton
includes chapters on the technique of string playing and
its development in Mendelssohn.

Houser, Roy. Catalogue of Chamber Music for Woodwind
Instruments. Bloomington: Indiana University School of
Music, n. d. Reprinted, New York: Da Capo Press,
1973. A very poor work; organization and procedures
poorly outlined; uses classifications such as "selective,"

"cumulative" and "classic" which are never defined; inconsistent presentation of information; lists much material which is either out-of-print or in manuscript.

Hughes, Rosemary. Haydn. New York: Farrar, Straus and Giroux, 1962. First part biographical, followed by chapters on musical characteristics, vocal works, keyboard works, etc. Appendices include a good catalog of works listed numerically with opus number, key, date, and pertinent remarks; bibliography; first appeared in print in 1950 published by J. M. Dent.

_____. Haydn String Quartets. (BBC Music Guides.) London: British Broadcasting Corporation, 1966. A helpful guide in simple language, the quality consistent with the other guides published by BBC and now obtainable through the University of Washington Press. The quartets are discussed chronologically in five chapters; index of works at end.

Hymanson, William. "Schoenberg's String Trio (1946)," Music Review 11 (1950): 184-94. An exhaustive analysis of the work.

Kerman, Joseph. The Beethoven Quartets. New York: Knopf, 1967. The July 1967 issue of Choice describes this as "a study in real depth, surpassing the work of Philip Radcliffe and contemporary in viewpoint ... " and as "essential for all students of chamber music." References to individual works are often scattered, but there is a detailed index of references to each.

Keys, Ivor. Brahms Chamber Music. (BBC Music Guides.) Seattle: University of Washington Press, 1974. Includes an overview and discussions of works by form; index; good blend of literary and musical comments; good analyses and music examples.

Kilburn, N. The Story of Chamber Music. (The Music Story Series, edited by Frederick J. Crowest.) London: Walter Scott Pub. Co.; New York: Scribner's, 1904. Another collector's item, especially for the chapters on chamber music institutions and concerts.

King, A. Hyatt. Mozart Chamber Music. (BBC Music Guides.) London: British Broadcasting Corporation, 1968. A very concise guide with an index of the works discussed.

Kinsky, Georg. Das Werk Beethoven; Thematisch-Biblio-
graphisches Verzeichnis seiner sämtlichen vollendeten
Kompositionen, edited by Hans Halm. Munich: G. Henle,
1955. This is a monumental work, finished by Hans
Halm after Kinsky's death. Its excellent organization
makes it easy to use. The works are divided into those
with opus numbers and those without, the latter receiving
the designation "WoO". Preceding each group is a list
of its contents giving titles, keys, dates of composition,
and page numbers. Full information is given for each
work, including an incipit for each movement and its
number of bars; also includes the publishing history of
the work, literature about it, and a concordance for other
catalogs and the Collected Edition of Beethoven's works.
The main part of the book is taken up with the systematic
classification; there are several appendices, including a
list of publishers by opus.

Köchel, Dr. Ludwig Ritter von. Chronologisch-thematisches
Verzeichnis sämtlicher Tonwerke Wolfgang Amade Mo-
zarts, 6th ed. , edited by Franz Giegling, Alexander
Weinmann, and Gerd Sievers. Wiesbaden: Breitkopf &
Härtel, 1965. This catalog has been in existence for
over 100 years; its most important revision was Alfred
Einstein's (third revision) in 1937--he maintained the
original chronological sequence and numbering system,
which had been in common use, but removed all spurious
works into appendices and inserted newly found works or
works which needed to be relocated in their correct places
with cross references from the old locations. There is
full publishing history, biographical facts, locations of
autographs, incipits of the movements, etc.

Koechel [sic] ABC, Chronological and Classified Listing of W. A.
Mozart's Works by Their Köchel Numbers, English adaptation by Robert Sabin. Wiesbaden: Breitkopf & Härtel,
1965. There is a table of contents arranged by form;
useful as a concordance to the Collected Edition of Mozart.

Kolneder, Walter. Anton Webern: An Introduction to His
Works, translated by Humphrey Searle. Berkeley: University of California Press, 1968. Extensive analysis
and comments; biographical sketch; bibliography and
catalog of works.

Kortsen, Bjarne. Contemporary Norwegian Chamber Music.
Fyllingsdalen, Norway: Bjarne Kortsen, 1971. A con-

tinuation and bringing-up-to-date of the author's Modern
Norwegian Chamber Music (see below).   Analyses of the
more important works with musical examples; adds 14
new composers; list of music on records and of literature
in English, Norwegian, and German.   An excellent contribution which might serve as a model for other national
groupings.

_____. Fartein Valen Life and Music.   Oslo: Johan
Grundt Tanum, 1965.   3 vols.   Volume one is biographical, two analyzes the music, and three consists solely
of the musical examples.   Kortsen, as a champion of
Valen, offers the first comprehensive study in English
and the first systematic investigation of the music.   Volume one includes the autobiography and correspondence
between Valen and Kortsen.

_____. Modern Norwegian Chamber Music.   Haugesund,
Norway: Bjarne Kortsen, 1965.   Reprinted, Bergen,
Norway: Bjarne Kortsen, 1969.   Survey includes a brief
history of chamber music in Norway, biographical sketches
for ten composers plus a list of works for each and a
detailed analysis of one representative composition for
each; there is a list of works arranged by number of
instruments and a discography.   See Kortsen's Contemporary..., above.

Króo, György.   A Guide to Bartók, translated by Ruth Pataki
and Maria Steiner; revised by Elisabeth West.   Budapest:
Corvina Press, 1974.   The pieces are arranged chronologically and described in a biographical setting; includes dates
and places of first performances and publishing information.

Laciar, Samuel L.   "The Chamber Music of Franz Schubert,"
Musical Quarterly 14 (1928):   515-38.   Each work treated
briefly, with the exception of the string quintet, which
receives a more detailed description.

Lam, Basil.   Beethoven String Quartets.   2 vols.   (BBC
Music Guides, edited by Lionel Salter.)   London: British
Broadcasting Corporation, 1975.   The first volume ends
with op. 74.   Contains brief analyses which are concise,
yet not too complex for the layman.

Landon, H. C. Robbins, ed.   The Mozart Companion.   London: Rockliff, 1956.   Articles by authorities such as
Otto Deutsch, Gerald Abraham, and Karl Geiringer; article
on chamber music by Hans Keller; index to music examples.

Library of Congress Catalog: Music--Books on Music and Sound Recordings. Washington, D. C. : Library of Congress, 1973-. A continuing and comprehensive bibliography which can be used as a tool for acquisition, reference, and research; includes scores, sheet music, libretti, books about music and musicians, and recordings. Title, author, and performer access; cross references; subject headings, based on Library of Congress Subject Headings List, are in a separate section at the end.

Loft, Abram. Violin and Keyboard: The Duo Repertoire. 2 vols. New York: Grossman, 1973. An approach from the performer's viewpoint which would be useful to teachers as well as students; some chapters focus on groups of sonatas, others on one composer or composition. Volume one is "From the Seventeenth Century to Mozart" and volume two is "From Beethoven to the Present." Extensive notes and bibliography; a list of editions used arranged by composer.

McColvin, Lionel R. Music in Public Libraries: A Guide to the Formation of a Music Library, with a Select List of Music and Musical Literature. London: Grafton, 1924. The list of compositions is coded to indicate which would be essential to a small library, which would be essential to a larger one, and which would be supplementary; other chapters on selection, cataloging, classification, binding, etc.

_____, and Reeves, Harold. Music Libraries: Their Organization and Contents, with a Bibliography of Music and Musical Literature. London: Grafton, 1938. The section on chamber music begins with trios for strings and ends with chamber music for winds; the list is classed according to the Dewey Decimal Classification; additional chapters include one on private collections; publishers and prices given.

Marliave, Joseph de. Beethoven Quartets. London: Oxford University Press, 1928. Preface by Gabriel Fauré; text divided into three periods; each quartet listed includes movement names and metronome markings; discusses performances, reviews, and life situations surrounding the compositions. Analyses emphasize the psychological rather than the technical.

Martynov, Ivan. Dmitrï Shostakovich: The Man and His Work, translated by T. Guralsky. New York: Philosophical Library, 1947. Reprinted, New York: Greenwood Press, 1969. No music examples or detailed analyses, yet the emphasis is on the works rather than the life of the composer.

Mason, Colin. "The Chamber Music of Milhaud," Musical Quarterly 43 (1957): 326-41. The author calls attention to the varied output of Milhaud, his style, accessibility, and similarity to Hindemith in certain ways.

_____. "Some Aspects of Hindemith's Chamber Music," Music and Letters 41 (1960): 150-55. Mason points out the composer's ingenious and imaginative variety of form, his conservatism of technique, and typical mannerisms.

Mason, Daniel Gregory. The Chamber Music of Brahms. New York: Macmillan, 1933. Meant for the general reader; discussions are of an aesthetic nature rather than a technical or theoretical one.

Meyer, Ernest H. English Chamber Music: The History of a Great Art. London: Lawrence & Wishart, 1946. Reprinted, New York: Da Capo Press, 1971. A well-written chronological survey which covers the Middle Ages to Purcell with chapter headings such as "The Medieval Background" and "Church Motet and Dance Tune, the Parents of English Chamber Music." The chapter "The Crisis" deals with the cleavage of aristocratic and popular taste between 1620 and 1642. Author's research abundantly documented; includes an appendix of the musical examples used.

Monelle, Raymond. "Bartók's Imagination in the Later Quartets," Music Review 31 (1970): 70-81. An enlightening article which points out Bartók's dialogical relationship with the past and discusses certain predilections such as the strong folk element.

Myers, Rollo H. Ravel: Life and Works. London: Gerald Duckworth, 1960. The section on works gives a general summary and then a survey by form; brief comments; includes selected discography and extensive bibliography of books and periodicals.

Norton, M. D. Herter. The Art of String Quartet Playing; Practice, Techniques, and Interpretation. New York: W. W. Norton, 1962. Unique in that it uses examples from the literature to illustrate points on style, phrasing,

tempo modifications, and rehearsing. Preface by Isaac
Stern; first published in 1952.

Opperman, Kalmen, comp. Repertory of the Clarinet. New
York: G. Ricordi, 1960. A very useful compilation
which is carefully prepared. Categories include methods,
texts, sonatas, unaccompanied solos, solos with piano
accompaniment and groupings ranging from two to fifteen.
Each grouping is subdivided according to instrumentation.

Ouellette, Fernand. Edgard Varèse, translated by Derek Colt-
man. New York: Orion Press, 1968. A chronological
arrangement with certain chapters devoted to particular
works; enormous bibliography of periodical articles from
1914 to 1966, with asterisks denoting the more significant
articles.

Page, Athol. Playing String Quartets. London: Longmans,
1964. Deals with technique and interpretation; quartets
arranged in chronological groups; unique in its comments
to the player on intonation problems, dynamics, and bowing; the playing time for each quartet that is discussed
is given.

Pellerite, James J. A Handbook of Literature for the Flute,
rev. ed. Bloomington, Ind. : Zālo Publications, 1965.
Literature for flute combinations only, graded on four
levels of difficulty; includes methods, orchestra studies,
and reference materials; comments on style and difficulties.

Peters, Harry B. , comp. The Literature of the Woodwind
Quintet. Metuchen, N. J. : Scarecrow Press, 1971. A
list giving length, quality of work and level of difficulty
in coded form; includes works with additional players;
arrangements within sections by composers.

Radcliffe, Philip. Beethoven's String Quartets. 1965. Paperback ed. , New York: Dutton, 1968. Opens with background material on relation of Beethoven to earlier quartet writers, particularly Haydn and Mozart; treats op.
18 and op. 59 as groups; views quartets from a broader
perspective than usual, comparing them to other works
of Beethoven and discussing their impact on other composers.

_____. Mendelssohn. (Master Musician Series.) London:
J. M. Dent, 1954. Reprinted, London: J. M. Dent,
1967; New York: Farrar, Straus and Giroux, 1967. A

survey of the chamber music can be found on pages 89 to 102.

Rasmussen, Mary. A Teacher's Guide to the Literature of Brass Instruments. Durham, N. H. : Brass Quarterly, 1964. An excellent evaluative guide; items graded for difficulty; contents include methods, books and articles, and recordings. The author has keen judgment and wit.

_____, and Mattran, Donald. A Teacher's Guide to the Literature of Woodwind Instruments. Durham, N. H. : Brass and Woodwind Quarterly, 1966. Excellent, succinct remarks; arranged by number of instruments with subdivisions by level of difficulty; includes repertoire for saxophone and recorder; lists ensembles for like instruments as well as mixed; helpful listing of all works discussed at the end of each chapter, arranged by composer and giving publishing information.

Redlich, Hans F. Alban Berg: The Man and His Music. New York: Abelard-Schuman, 1957. Divided into sections on the music and the life. The Appendix section includes Schoenberg's writing on Berg, Berg's lecture on Wozzeck, a catalog of works, and a discography.

_____. "Bruckner and Brahms Quintets in F," Music and Letters 36 (1965): 253-58. Author discusses striking parallels.

Reich, Willi. Schoenberg: A Critical Biography, translated by Leo Black. New York: Praeger, 1971. Includes a list of works, a bibliography, and appendices, the first of which is a self-analysis by the composer.

Richter, Johannes Friedrich. Kammermusik-Katalog. Leipzig: Friedrich Hofmeister, 1960. This is the 1944-1958 continuation of the Altmann chamber-music catalog found earlier in this list; same arrangement as the Altmann; useful for an overview of repertoire available at that time.

Risdon, Howard. Musical Literature for the Bassoon: A Compilation of Music for the Bassoon and as an Instrument in Ensemble. Seattle: Berdon, 1963. Includes out-of-print music; employs an unnecessarily complex code; preparation seems somewhat inadequate, which is unfortunate, considering the need for such a compilation.

Riseling, Robert A. "Motivic Structure in Beethoven's Late

Quartets," in Paul A. Pisk: Essays in His Honor, edited by John Glowacki. Austin: College of Fine Arts, University of Texas, 1966. The author is concerned not with formal structure but thematic process and three forces that shape thematic material: organic relationships of simple motivic cells, rhythmical constructions, extension of the spatial concept of the quartet idiom. The article is found on pages 141-62.

Robertson, Alec, ed. Chamber Music. 1957. Reprinted, London: Penguin, 1963. Deals with individual composers, groupings by form, and composers by country; select bibliography; index of composers.

Rowland-Jones, A. Recorder Technique. London: Oxford University Press, 1959. Chapter two and the supplement deal with the repertoire.

Sansone, Lorenzo. French Horn Music Literature. New York: Sansone Musical Instruments, 1962. Includes many obscure compositions; however, it lacks publishing information and there is no attempt at accuracy, consistency, or thoroughness.

Schenk, Erich. The Trio Sonata Outside Italy, translated by Robert Kolben. (Vol. 42 of Anthology of Music: A Collection of Complete Musical Examples Illustrating the History of Music, edited by K. G. Fellerer.) Cologne: Arno Volk Verlag, 1970. An excellent survey, by country, of Early Baroque, Late Baroque, Style Galant, Rococo and Sentimental style; well-produced musical examples; helpful list of reprints of the literature as well as of the music; lengthy bibliography. Also recommended is volume 20 in the series, The Italian Trio Sonata, also by Erich Schenk.

Scherman, Thomas K., and Biancolli, Louis, eds. The Beethoven Companion. Garden City, N. Y.: Doubleday, 1972. The excellent outline in the Table of Contents indicates title, opus number, source of analysis, and page number; analytical essays are divided by period, with biographical material preceding analyses; section on chamber music divided into chamber music with piano and chamber music without piano.

Schmieder, Wolfgang. Thematisch-systematisches Verzeichnis der musikalischen Werke von Johann Sebastian Bach, Bach-Werke-Verzeichnis (BWV). Leipzig: Breitkopf &

Härtel, 1950. A monumental undertaking; divides by
vocal and instrumental; each part systematically classified; includes concordance for the Gesellschaft Collected
Edition.

Schwann-I, Record and Tape Guide. Boston: W. Schwann,
1949-. Changes name from time to time; published
monthly on a non-subscription basis; sections on new
recordings, electronic music, collections, musicals,
movie music, etc. The classical section, arranged by
composer and sub-divided by form, gives composer's
dates, opus numbers and keys of the individual works,
thematic numbers if available, and cross references to
works on the other side of the disc. Other publications
include a supplement twice a year which contains mon-
aural recordings and folk, a children's records catalog,
and a Christmas catalog. An artist issue is also published annually.

Sourek, Otakar. The Chamber Music of Antonín Dvořák,
translated by Roberta Finlayson Samsour. Prague: Artia, n. d. Arrangement by number of instruments starting
with six and ending with two; the introduction relates
Dvořák's life to his works; details given for first performances, first publications, and durations of each work;
each composition treated generally and then in more analytical detail.

Stevens, Halsey. The Life and Music of Béla Bartók, rev.
ed. London and New York: Oxford University Press,
1953, 1964. Paperback ed. , 1967. Author states that
the book is concerned primarily with the music approached
from both the analytical and the critical points of view,
and that Part I, the biographical study, is not exhaustive
or definitive. Part II is divided into categories by form
--the string quartets make up the third category and the
rest of the chamber music makes up the fourth. Music
discussed chronologically; there is a detailed chronological
list of works with titles in English and Hungarian, plus
an impressive bibliography of books and articles written
by Bartók as well as books, articles, and references in
books and articles about him.

Stuckenschmidt, H. H. Maurice Ravel: Variations on His
Life and Work, translated by Samuel R. Rosenbaum.
Philadelphia: Chilton Book Co. , 1968. A descriptive
treatment of the artistic influences and events in Ravel's
life, with little analysis.

Tovey, Donald Francis. <u>Essays and Lectures on Music.</u>
London: Oxford University Press, 1949. The author's
output on chamber music is extensive; here he includes
chapters on the chamber music of Haydn, Schubert,
Brahms, Beethoven, and Dohnányi.

_____. <u>Essays in Musical Analysis: Chamber Music.</u>
London: Oxford University Press, 1944. A collection
of writings from 1900 to 1936 in which Tovey discusses
the continuo period and the central classics of the sonata
style.

Truscott, Harold. <u>Beethoven's Late String Quartets.</u> London: Dobson, 1968. A listening guide prepared for a
1964 series of broadcasts; the author defends the accessibility of the late quartets and also the logic of the
works as examples of classical sonata structure rather
than as fantasias. The narrative style is somewhat awkward.

_____. "Schubert's String Quartet in G major," <u>Music</u>
<u>Review</u> 20 (1959): 119-45. A detailed discussion.

Ujfalussy, József. <u>Béla Bartók,</u> translated by Ruth Pataki;
translation revised by Elisabeth West. Budapest: Corvina, 1971. Topics range from "Childhood and Student
Years" to "Folk Music Inspiration and Its First Great
Creative Products." Appendices include survey of major
events in life of composer, chronological list of works,
instrumentation, dedication, and publishing information.

Ulrich, Homer. <u>Chamber Music: The Growth and Practice</u>
<u>of an Intimate Art.</u> New York: Columbia University
Press, 1948. An excellent survey with several chapters
devoted to the backgrounds and early forms of chamber
music; extensive classified bibliography.

Unverricht, Hubert. <u>Chamber Music,</u> translated by A. C.
Howie. (Vol. 46 of <u>Anthology of Music: A Collection</u>
<u>of Complete Musical Examples Illustrating the History</u>
<u>of Music,</u> edited by K. G. Fellerer.) Cologne: Arno
Volk Verlag, 1975. In the Foreword the author points
out the neglect of many genres and the sporadic consider-
ation of the chamber music of individual composers.
There are five sections: a survey of chamber music and
its history; contemporary tendencies; reproduced scores
of either entire movements or entire works; new editions
of chamber music works in individual Denkmäler volumes

and in volumes forming part of a series; heavily documented information on sources, plus editorial remarks;
31 chamber music bibliographies included in the general
music bibliography.

Vester, Franz. <u>Flute Repertoire Catalogue: 10,000 Titles.</u>
London: Musica Rara, 1967. Various sections on literature written on the flute, methods, orchestral studies,
flute and voice combinations, etc. The section on instrumental chamber music is divided by combinations; publishing information is provided.

Voxman, Himie, and Merriman, Lyle. <u>Woodwind Ensemble</u>
<u>Music Guide.</u> Evanston, Ill. : The Instrumentalist, 1973.
Good current source; the information is derived from
catalogs of 262 publishers; contents grouped by number,
up to 13 players.

Weerts, Richard K. , comp. <u>Original Manuscript Music for</u>
<u>Wind and Percussion Instruments.</u> Ann Arbor, Mich. :
National Association of College Wind and Percussion Instructors, 1964. This is a revision of the original 1958-
59 list; now includes over 400 compositions; lists music
for either woodwind, brass, or percussion ensemble, but
no mixed groups; addresses supplied for composers and/
or publishers.

Westrup, J. A. <u>Schubert Chamber Music.</u> (BBC Music
Guides.) Seattle: University of Washington Press, 1969.
Author touches on social circumstances of Schubert's
works; candid appraisals of what author considers weak-
nesses or inconsistencies in the works; the schemes of
movements and outlines of form given for the major compositions. A classed index gives opus numbers, Deutsch
numbers, dates of composition and publication, and Gesam-
tausgaben (Complete Edition) numbers and pages.

Whittall, Arnold. <u>Schoenberg Chamber Music.</u> (BBC Music
Guides.) Seattle: University of Washington Press, 1972.
An essay with a contents list at the beginning, indicating
on which page each work is discussed; a good, concen-
trated presentation.

Wilkins, Wayne, ed. and comp. <u>The Index of Bassoon Music</u>
<u>including the Index of Baroque Trio Sonatas.</u> Magnolia,
Ark. : The Music Register, 1976. Includes methods,
studies, duets, trios, etc. , up to ten instruments. A

composer arrangement giving title, instrumentation, key, opus number, and publisher. Publisher list includes agents and gives addresses. Indices available for flute, oboe, violin with strings, violin with winds, and viola.

_____, ed. and comp. The Index of Clarinet Music. Magnolia, Ark. : The Music Register, 1975. Current source for publishers' addresses; classified list by number, subdivided by instrumentation; separate sections for combinations with piano and those without; the author is compiling other indices for various wind and string instruments.

Winterfield, Linde Höffer v. Handbuch der Blockflöten-Literatur. Berlin: Bote & Bock, 1959. An alphabetical list of recorder literature by title and composer; main section classified by instrumentation; separate sections on literature on the recorder and music for Christmas.

Yoell, John H. The Nordic Sound. Boston: Crescendo, 1974. Part II, "Composers Gallery" includes descriptions of the music of Berwald, Grieg, Nielsen, Riisager, and Valen. A useful tool in light of the paucity of material in English on Scandinavian music and musicians.

DIRECTORY OF PUBLISHERS

AMP see Associated Music Publishers

Artia see Boosey & Hawkes

Associated Music Publishers
48-02 48th Ave.
Woodside, NY 11377

Augener see Galaxy

Bärenreiter Verlag
Heinrich-Schütz-Allee 29
3500 Kassel-Wilhelmshöhe,
    Germany
    see also Boonin;
        Magnamusic-Baton;
        Schirmer

M. Baron Co.
Box 149
Oyster Bay, NY 11771

Belmont Music Publishers
PO Box 49961
Los Angeles, CA 90049

Belwin-Mills, Inc.
25 Deshon Drive
Melville, NY 11746

Bomart see Associated Music Publishers

Joseph Boonin, Inc.
PO Box 2124
South Hackensack, NJ 07606

Boosey & Hawkes
Box 130
Oceanside, NY 11572

Boston Music Company
    see Frank

Bote & Bock see Associated Music Publishers

Breitkopf & Härtel see Associated Music Publishers; Alexander Broude

Broadcast Music see Associated Music Publishers

Alexander Broude
225 West 57th St.
New York, NY 10019

Broude Brothers, Ltd.
56 W. 45th St.
New York, NY 10036

J. & W. Chester, Ltd.
Eagle Court
London EC 1M, England
    see also Magnamusic-Baton

Costallat see Presser

Cundy-Bettoney see Fischer

167

J. Curwen & Sons, Ltd.
24 Berners St.
W1 London, England
see also Schirmer

Dan Fog see Samfundet
til Udgivelse Dansk
Musik

Delkas see Leeds

Deutscher Verlag für Musik
see Alexander Broude

Pietro Diero
133 Seventh Ave.
New York, NY 10014

Ludwig Doblinger Verlag
see Associated
Music Publishers

Donemus see Peters

Durand & Cie see Presser

Edition Musicus
PO Box 1341
Stamford, CT 06904

Henri Elkan
1316 Walnut St.
Philadelphia, PA 19107

Engstrøm & Sødring
Palaisgade 6
Copenhagen K, Denmark
see also Peters

Max Eschig see Associated
Music Publishers

Eulenberg see Peters

Carl Fischer, Inc.
56 Cooper Square
New York, NY 10003

Frank Distributing Corp.
116 Boylston St.
Boston, MA 02116

Galaxy Music Corporation
2121 Broadway
New York, NY 10023

Carl Gehrmans Musikförlag
Vasagaten 46
Stockholm 1, Sweden
see also Boosey; Elkan-
Vogel; Southern
Music

Hamelle & Cie see Pres-
ser

Wilhelm Hansen Musik-
Forlag see Magna-
music-Baton

Heinrichshofen's Verlag
see Peters

G. Henle Verlag
Schongauerstrasse 24
8 Munich 70, West Germany
see also Magnamusic-
Baton

Heugel & Cie see Presser

Hinrichsen see Peters

Friedrich Hofmeister see
Alexander Broude

Hortus Musicus see Bär-
enreiter; Boonin; Mag-
namusic-Baton

International Music Com-
pany
511 Fifth Ave.
New York, NY 10017

Edwin F. Kalmus
PO Box 1007
Opa-Locka, FL 33054

Robert King Music
112A Main Street
North Easton, MA 02356

Lea see Presser

Alphonse Leduc
175 rue St. Honoré
Paris, France
    see also Baron; Boonin;
      Presser; Southern
      Music (Texas)

Leeds Music Corp. see
    Music Corporation of
    America

F. E. C. Leuckart see
    Associated Music Pub-
    lishers

Robert Lienau Musikverlag
    see Peters

Collection Litolff see
    Peters

Harald Lyche & Co.
Kongensgate 2
Oslo, Norway
    see also Peters

MCA see Music Corpo-
    ration of America

MZK see Music Pub-
    lishers of the USSR

Magnamusic-Baton, Inc.
10370 Page Industrial Blvd.
St. Louis, MO 63132

Edward B. Marks see
    Belwin-Mills

McGinnis & Marx see
    Diero

Mills Music, Inc. see
    Belwin-Mills

Moeck see Belwin;
    Magnamusic-Baton
    (for 20th-century
    music)

Music Publishers Holding
    Corp.
619 W. 54th St.
New York, NY 10019

Music Publishers of the
    USSR see Music
    Corporation of Amer-
    ica

Musica Rara
2 Great Marlborough St.
London W1, England
    see also Rubank

Nagels Verlag see Boon-
    in; Magnamusic-
    Baton

New Music Edition see
    Presser

Norsk Musikforlag see
    Associated Music
    Publishers; Magna-
    music-Baton

Novello
PO Box 1811
Trenton, NJ 08607

Edition de l'Oiseau-Lyre
122 rue de Grenelle
Paris 9, France
    see also Broude
      Brothers

Oxford University Press
200 Madison Ave.
New York, NY 10016

Patterson's Publications, Ltd.
36 Wigmore St.
London W1, England
    see also Fischer

Peer International Corp.
1740 Broadway
New York, NY 10019
    see also Southern Music

C. F. Peters Corp.
373 Park Ave. South
New York, NY 10016

Theodore Presser Co.
Presser Place
Bryn Mawr, PA 19010

Pro Art Publications, Inc.
Box 234
Westbury, NY 11590

G. Ricordi & Co.
16 W. 61st St.
New York, NY 10023
    see also Belwin-Mills;
        Fischer

Rubank, Inc.
16215 NW 15th St.
Miami, FL 33169

Salabert
575 Madison Ave.
New York, NY 10022

Samfundet til Udgivelse
    Dansk Musik see
    Peters

G. Schirmer
866 Third Ave.
New York, NY 10022

B. Schott's Söhne
Weihergarten 5
65 Mainz, Germany
    see also Belwin-
        Mills; Boonin;
        Magnamusic-Baton

Hans Sikorski Musikverlag
    see Belwin-Mills

N. Simrock see Asso-
    ciated Music Publishers

Southern Music
1740 Broadway
New York, NY 10019

Southern Music (Texas)
1100 Broadway
San Antonio, Tx 78206

Stainer & Bell, Ltd.
148 Charing Cross Rd.
London WC2, England
    see also Galaxy

Edition Suecia/Stockholm
    Föreningen Svenska
    Tonsättare see
    Gehrmans

Edizioni Suvini Zerboni
    see Music Corporation
    of America

UE see Universal Edition

Union Musical Espanola
    see Baron

Universal Edition see
    Boonin

Valley Press (New Valley
    Music Press of Smith
    College)
Sage Hall
Northampton, MA 01060

Chr. Friedrich Vieweg see
    Peters

WIM see Western Inter-
    national

Weaner-Levant
[no address available]

Western International
2859 Holt Ave.
Los Angeles, CA 90034

Wilhelm Zimmermann Musik-
    verlag see Peters

M. Witmark & Sons see
    Music Publishers Hold-
    ing Company

POPULAR TITLE INDEX

COMPOSER INDEX